Every
Dream *is about*
the Dreamer

Barbara Condron
D.M., D.D., B.J.

SOM Publishing
Windyville, Missouri 65783 U.S.A.

By the same author

Spiritual Renaissance:
 Elevating Your Consciousness for the Common Good

First Opinion: Wholistic Health Care in the 21st Century

The Work of the Soul

The Dreamer's Dictionary

The Bible Interpreted in Dream Symbols

Uncommon Knowledge

Kundalini Rising

Remembering Atlantis: History of the World Vol. 1

How to Raise an Indigo Child

Peacemaking: 9 Lessons for Changing Yourself,
  Your Relationships, and Your World

The Wisdom of Solomon
  Infinite Possibilities in Finite Experiences Book IV

© September, 2004
by the School of Metaphysics No. 100174

Cover Art by Michelle Noe
Sketches by Chris Sheehan

ISBN: 0-944386-27-x
Library of Congress Control Number: 2004095396

PRINTED IN THE UNITED STATES OF AMERICA

If you desire to learn more about the research and
teachings in this book, write to School of Metaphysics
World Headquarters, Windyville, Missouri 65783.
Or call us at 417-345-8411.
Visit us on the Internet at www.som.org
or www.dreamschool.org

In decades of research spanning the globe, students and teachers at the School of Metaphysics have found there are two guiding principles, applicable universally, for dreaming.

1 Every dream is about the dreamer.

2 Every one and every thing in the dream is the dreamer.

This book is about both.

C^{The}ontents

The Language of our Dreams

When the photographer, filming the world leaders gathered during the 50th anniversary of the United Nations, wanted his subjects to smile what did he say?

Nothing.

What did he do?

He unveiled a yellow circle with a smiling face. The photographer used an image -- a picture beyond a 1000 words -- that would elicit the response he desired.

In a crowded airport, people speaking a dozen different languages rely on a simple system of pictures to communicate directions and locations -- a shaded silhouette of a male or female on the door identifies separate facilities for the two sexes, a picture of a subway car denotes a tram depot, a telephone and an arrow mark the way to communication services. Each airline also has its unique picture logo which makes it readily recognizable.

When Internet users send electronic mail they use "emoticons" to convey their emotional attitude. Thus if someone is smiling you'll see :-) . If they are kidding: ;-) . If they're laughing: :-D. How do these punctuation marks convey the thought? Turn the page 90° to the right. What do you see? You're probably :-& which means tongue-tied! It's a clever system, and it works for people across the globe because it uses universally understandable pictures.

The airport pictures, the photographer's smiling face, and computer emoticons illustrate how pictures or images are currently used as a universal means of communication. Far from being a new means of thought transference, images are proving to be at the heart of the oldest language known to man, a language researchers at the School of Metaphysics in the United States have named the Universal Language of Mind. Researchers at the not-for-profit educational institute have decoded the language by investigating the nature of consciousness and the development of human potential. Our research unites philosophy and science, art and technology. It spans three decades and involves millions of people, ages six to eighty-six, from all walks of life and on six continents. Much of the experiential research centers on the dreaming mind, the inner mind.

The Small Voice with the Power

Everyone realizes "it" exists. And everyone reaps the benefits of its capabilities.

"It" is the small voice that urges you to go ahead and introduce yourself to the person who you later marry, or the queasy feeling in the pit of your stomach that tells you to take a different flight and serendipitously so, or the skill that enables you to convince your children that you have eyes in the back of your head. It is the part of self where out-of-body experiences occur, or where we "read" the "vibes" in a room, or where we go when we sleep each night, thus our acute interest in dream states.

"It" is what SOM researchers describe as the subconscious part of mind. Through experiential and empirical research, my colleagues and I have made some startling discoveries in the area of mind-body relativity,

2

not the least of which is the study of an outstanding separation between the human mind and the body's brain. The mind and the body are not, as is widely believed, one and the same. Our findings repeatedly point to a distinct difference between these two components of man.

This has led us to identify the mind as the individual's intelligence and creative faculty that clearly on some level exist independently of the physical body. The brain is an organ of the body; albeit a sophisticated and as yet unreplicated organ, but no more fascinating than a liver with its hundreds of functions absolutely essential for life or the electro-chemical precision of a heart that beats 2,838,240,000 times throughout a 75 year life span or a reproductive system that houses, nurtures, and births a whole and complete offspring of two genetically different parents. The mind utilizes the body and brain for experiencing and learning in the physical plane. The relationship of mind to body is similar to that of a driver to an automobile. The relationship of mind to brain is similar to the relationship of a computer programmer to a computer. We expect this revolutionary concept to be widely accepted and used in the coming millennium with outstanding results.

The recognition of the mind-body separation has encouraged us to explore the inner realms of mind, what we term the subconscious mind. This is not to be confused with psychological ideas of the "unconscious mind" which describe that of which we are not, or refuse to be, aware. In our research subconscious mind describes a vibrant, re-creative part of the whole self; a storehouse of understandings referred to often as the soul. Subconscious activities – be they described as instinct, intuition, or conscience – operate for most people below the surface of the outer, busy awake consciousness. Thus most people are unconscious of the subconscious part of mind.

The subconscious mind is not a lesser part of Self. It is different from the outer waking consciousness---the conscious mind which works directly with the physical body and brain. The power of the conscious mind is reasoning which is the ability to use memory, attention, and imagination to discern truth. The power of the subconscious mind is intuition; the direct grasp of truth from understandings already gleaned through experience and which are universally applicable.

It's like the difference between the way a typical male and a typical female find the same destination. He will tend to rely upon directions including maps and compass points. He wants to hear, "Go east on Broadway. Turn north at First Street, go two blocks." But she will say, "Stay on the road to the left of the park. Turn right before the cathedral but after the rose garden entrance. You can't miss it," because she tends to rely upon images and landmarks for location. Each are capable of achieving the same goal by sometimes entirely different means.

Because males and females tend to approach everything in life differently there is attraction between the sexes. Together they can create much more than when alone. The same is true of the conscious mind and subconscious mind; they create more together than alone. Each part of mind performs entirely different functions, reasoning and intuition, necessary for a whole self.

Pillow Talk

Dreaming is the most commonly recognized means that the inner mind communicates to the outer mind. The idea that dreams are a communication from beyond the physical existence is not new. For thousands of years mankind has been captivated and perplexed by memories of experiences arising when his physical consciousness is at rest. These memories have become an integral part of every culture on this planet.

Historical records and literature are filled with accounts of dreaming. Mary Shelley's nightmare becomes her novel about man as creator: <u>Frankenstein</u>. Abraham Lincoln's dream foretells his death. Jacob of the Biblical *Old Testament* dreams of a stairway to Heaven. Dorothy dreams of a journey to a land called Oz. In every case man has searched for a reason for these phenomena. Common to them all is the recognition that night time dreams are a form of communication.

What is new in our research is the understanding of the universal principles that empower that communication. For most people, sleeping is the only time their conscious, waking minds are still enough to possibly attend to what the inner subconscious mind has to say. Remembering your dreams, in essence actively listening to your own subconscious mind, is very much like having a conversation with your best friend. It requires giving and receiving.

When you're distracted, not paying attention to your friend, he may need to raise his voice to get your attention. Nightmares are the way your subconscious mind "raises its voice" to capture your conscious attention.

When you keep interrupting your friend, she may stop talking to you or she may find herself endlessly repeating what she has said. Recurring dreams are the means your subconscious mind uses to repeat its unheeded messages.

When you do all the talking and your friend has little opportunity to say anything, you know only about yourself and nothing about your friend. So it is when you refuse to heed your dreams; you learn nothing about your inner Self.

The tendency to ignore the importance of dreams is the foundation of one of the most widely accepted myths in Western culture today. Many erroneously believe that dreams are irrevocably and solely personal. They like to believe their dreams mean whatever they want them to mean. This is tantamount to believing that other people think only what you want them to think which of course is not true. Your subconscious mind has something to contribute, something worthy of your conscious mind's attention. Listening to what your subconscious mind has to say about your state of awareness is like gaining feedback from your best friend. Since the subconscious mind has the power to directly grasp the truth the benefit to you can be priceless.

The Oldest Language Known to Man

It is from the dream research that a universal language of mind has surfaced. This language is not man-made as is English, Spanish, or Japanese. It was not conceived by one person, one mind, but rather by a group of minds or humanity. Just as each nation has its physical language for the communication of ideas and perceptions so dreams are conveyed in the language spoken by a group of minds. What SOM researchers have named Universal Language of Mind is this language. Thus the oldest language known to man becomes the "new" language of the next millennium.

The a, b, c's of the Universal Language of Mind -- the symbols -- are universal. They mean the same thing for everyone: rich and poor, young and old, regardless of race, creed or religious faith. These symbols or images appear in all Holy scriptures, parables, myths, and even fairy tales. The names of characters differ and the outward trappings of story lines may vary, but the images are comparable. Shakespeare's Hamlet, Milton's Dante, The Bible's King Solomon, the Bhagavad Gita's Arjuna, Aladdin, Cinderella, or Alice in Wonderland. They all are universally understandable. This is what makes their stories enduring classics. They transcend time, space, and culture.

When anyone, anytime, anywhere can derive meaning from a story, it has been created in the Universal Language of Mind. This language is universal because it transcends physical differences of language, culture, ideology. This is the language used on the level of the subconscious mind or soul where all of mankind is connected. We all have universal desires, all of us have universal urges, all of us have the same reason for being here despite all of our outward physical differences. Learning the language your inner mind speaks frees you to open your conscious mind to move beyond diversity and its limitations.

Imagine, trying to converse with someone who speaks a different language! You would be acting out your thoughts, in essence creating pictures, trying to make each other understand what you are saying. As you will find in your waking conversations with others, it is a definite asset to speak the same language. Between people this makes for an easy way to share thoughts. Between the conscious mind and the subconscious mind speaking the same language ensures meaningful communication.

Dreams are Myths with Personal Morals

Like parables and myths, every dream tells a story about the dreamer often teaching a lesson to be discerned and applied by the dreamer. The Universal Language of Mind becomes the Rosetta Stone that will unlock the meaning of your dreams. Dreams offer insights into the state of your awareness. They are communicated in universal symbols and are personally relevant to you, the dreamer. The characters and action in your dream present a symbolic story about you and for you. When interpreted, dreams teach us in much the same way a fable or parable presents a message or lesson to be learned. The lesson is learned when it is applied in the dreamer's life.

Applying the Truth revealed in dreams causes new ways of thinking and acting, promoting a change and growth in your awareness. For instance, you dream that you are running down a long dark street. Something is chasing after you but you don't look back to see what it is. When you get to the end of the street there is nowhere to go. This dream indicates you are avoiding the acknowledgement of an aspect or part of your Self. In the dream you do not even look to see what is motivating you to run informing you that you are unaware of your own intentions in life. Through the dream images, your subconscious mind is telling you that the result in your waking life is similar to the dead-end reached in the dream; your choices are significantly limited.

If you've had this kind of dream, you will benefit from admitting the many opportunities open to you and setting goals for a lifestyle you find worthy of pursuing. In this way you respond to the Truth revealed in the dream.

We at the School of Metaphysics believe mankind is now on the threshold of profound evolution and spiritual revelation. The interpretation of dreams, once the territory of spiritual leaders only, is becoming the individual's domain as each person reaches into his own spiritual nature seeking the cause for what he experiences---the source of his existence.

The ability to understand the messages received in dreams is quickly being recognized as the link between the physically visible and invisible universes of man. Night time dreams are easily the most accessible way to understand and establish inner communication as long as the waking mind is willing to learn the language used by the inner mind which provides the dream.

When understood, dream images provide significant feedback concerning the dreamer's spiritual, mental, emotional, and physical state of being. Every dream is about the dreamer. Being attentive and informed about your dream states can resolve problems, enhance creativity, and accelerate learning.

Our research indicates all dreams, including flying dreams, nightmares, and recurring dreams, are relevant messages to and about the dreamer. By sharing our findings it is our hope that we can in time raise an enlightened generation. Imagine --- a generation who knows the value of their dreams and how to use their inner wisdom to lead fulfilling and productive lives for themselves and all of humanity. The possibilities for progress are infinite.

Toward this end, the School of Metaphysics annually sponsors the National Dream Hotline® the last weekend in April. For 54 continuous hours, faculty mann phone lines to share research findings and to answer callers' questions about their dreams. We answer questions from men and women, young and old, novice and adept. Calls come from across the United States and Canada, from Madrid to Hong Kong to South Africa.

SOM also maintains two websites: www.som.org and www.dreamschool.org. The latter is devoted solely to dream study, research, and awareness. For more about the School of Metaphysics visit these sites or contact us at world headquarters in Windyville, Missouri USA.

10

Most Common Symbols Appearing in Dreams*

and their translation in the
Universal Language of Mind

1] *Animals* represent habits. Animals function from instinct, reacting to pleasure or pain. Having differing degrees of memory and the ability for attention, animals lack the evolutionary development including sufficient brain capacity needed for the imagination to operate. Most animals in a dream will represent the dreamer's habits.

2] *Baby* is a new idea. A child is the result of the uniting of a male and female. In the Universal Language of Mind, this represents the cooperative use of aggressive and receptive principles to create something new.

3] *Clothes* signify how the dreamer is expressing Self. Clothes indicate the part of self others view. Many cultures describe the three-fold nature of self as the person we show to others, the person we believe ourselves to be, and the person we truly are. Clothes signify what we allow others to see.

4] *Death* symbolizes change. Death in a dream is frightening to most dreamers because they lack understanding of the nature of physical life and death. For the aware thinker, the physical life is known as a temporary existence for the soul. The French philosopher Voltaire said centuries ago, "It is no more surprising to be born twice than once, everything in nature is resurrection." In the Universal Language of Mind, death signifies a change from one state of being to another.

5] *Food* represents knowledge. Physically food nourishes the body. Mentally knowledge nourishes the mind, thus the old adage "food for thought".

6] *House* represents the dreamer's mind. The mind is comprised of three major divisions: conscious, subconscious, and superconscious. Within these divisions are a total of seven levels of consciousness. A house symbolizes the mind. The floors of the house represent different part of mind, the activity signifies how the dreamer is using this structure for thinking.

7] *Marriage* symbolizes a commitment between the conscious mind and the subconscious mind for fulfillment of desires. Marriage is the union of a male and female. In the language of mind, marriage symbolizes the commitment between the conscious and subconscious minds. In order for this commitment to occur there must be a conscious willingness for cooperation with the inner Self. This type of dream indicates the initiation of a new awareness for the dreamer.

12

8] *Vehicles* represent a means for giving and receiving experiences. Small vehicles such as a car or boat represent the dreamer's physical body. Large vehicles [busses, large airplanes, ships] symbolize the dreamer's choice of vehicles [such as an organization, company, church] for experiencing what physical life affords. The use of the vehicle will give indications of the type of experience being related in the dream message. For instance an ambulance will indicate a need for healing in the giving and receiving of experience, a police car will signify the need for discipline in experiences.

9] *Water* represents conscious life experiences. Physical water is essential to life. In the Universal Language of mind, water symbolizes the experience in the physical level of consciousness. These are the everyday, waking, interactions, situations and circumstances that arise bringing opportunities for enrichment.

10] *Money* represents exchange of value. How the money is being used in the dream will indicate what is being valued. For instance, if money is being used to buy a house this will symbolize the value the dreamer places upon his own mind; if it is being invested for future use it will indicate the wealth derived from experiences which is permanent understanding.

*From **The Dreamer's Dictionary** by Dr. Barbara Condron,
SOM Publishing.*

Since www.dreamschool.org was launched in 1998,
we at the School of Metaphysics (SOM)
have interpreted thousands of dreams
from people around the world.
This vast body of research supports the existence of
a Universal Language of Mind,
a language spoken by a group of intelligent beings
known as humans, who SOM has been teaching since 1973.

Because these dreams come from dreamers on almost
every continent, they reflect back to us who we are
and how we can grow as a race into our potential.
They tell us that as a planet we are in the midst
of constant change, often unconscious of the cause
or where the change will lead. They also tell us that
we desire harmony with ourselves and with each other,
and that we possess the qualities necessary to create
anything we imagine. They tell us that we are
experiencing in increasing numbers the limitless
dimensions of consciousness beyond the physical world and
in that way these dreams give us a preview of what is to
come.

The dreams assembled here are as unique
to the dreamer as they are commonplace to us all. And
that, alone, says quite a bit about the importance of
dreaming in our lives.

*What we dream about
and what it means*

e-mail interpretations of dreams

The dreams in this book were chosen from the hundreds of e-mails sent to the School of Metaphysics in a year's time. They represent people of all backgrounds and ages, as well as several countries. The e-mails appear here in the form they were sent, which sometimes includes spelling or grammatical errors. Where this might make the dream difficult to read or understand, adjustments have been made. Each correspondence is set apart from interpretations by lines with the dreams italicized. Interpretations follow with suggestions for responsive action to the dream message. These dreams appear because they represent a wide spectrum of the universal dreaming experience. If you have questions about dream content not included here there are several actions you can take:

1) send your dream to us at
dreams@dreamschool.org

2) write to us as School of Metaphysics
World Headquarters, Windyville, MO 65783
or

3) look for similar dreams at
www.dreamschool.org

Message in a Dream

This is the first time I am writing. I heard about you on the radio one day and was very interested. I had a dream about 3 years ago that is still so vivid in my mind.

In the dream, *my sister-in-law told me that she had the power to communicate with the dead. She told me that her mother, (my mother-in-law) had a message for me. She said to tell me that Everything was going to be o.k. and not to worry anymore.*

I really want to know what this means. I have a son who is developmentally disabled. My mother in law died when my son was four years old. He is now 17 yrs. old. Please help me understand this.
Thanks, from a concerned, loving mom

Response

Our dreams use the people, places, and things in our lives to tell us a story about us. The story is symbolic and has personal meaning that can help us live our lives. Although dreams can demonstrate other sub-conscious capabilities like precognition or visitation, this dream does not indicate that occurring. This dream is a message for you about you from your own inner self.

Your sister-in-law represents a familiar aspect of you that holds onto the past. During the day before you had this dream you were thinking in old ways – that you had changed but now were slipping back into. Your connection with superconscious tells you to keep your attention in present rather than the future.

Love Letter

I had a dream *I was sleeping and my little sister woke me up and gave me an open letter. It was from someone that I fell in love with in September and he moved away in December. He wrote me once. But it was just basic information about what he had been doing. I wrote him and I told him how I felt about him. But he never wrote back. The letter was four or five pages long. It was written in different colors of ink. At the top of one of the pages it said something similar to "I know that you like me". When you turn the page over at the top it said "We are partners".*

There was more information in the letters but that is the only words I remember. I would like an interpretation. Thank you for your time.
S, female

Response

Dreams offer insights into the state of your awareness. When interpreting your own dreams there are two universally true principles to keep in mind:

1. Every dream is about the dreamer.

2. Every person, place and thing in the dream represents the dreamer.

A dream is a message from your inner self.

Sleeping in the dream is a symbol of a loss of awareness and will. You don't give your physical age, but we wouldn't be surprised if you are physically young. This dream is addressing the feelings of separation that arise as we age. Since we are not actively taught to keep the connection between the inner and outer, the subconscious and conscious minds, over time the outer ego stimulates the conscious mind toward dominance. This dream message is a commentary on this all too common death of awareness.

The aspect of yourself symbolized by your little sister plays an important part in this dream message. That conscious aspect is the part of you that is establishing the communication between yourself and your subconscious mind (symbolized by the boy). You believe there is separation from your subconscious mind, the part of yourself your sister represents knows better.

If you have a desire to learn more about dream interpretation, check out the classes and lectures here at dreamschool. In addition **The Dreamer's Dictionary** (by Dr. Barbara Condron) has a wealth of information about understanding the symbols in the Universal Language of Mind. It is available for $15 at all fine bookstores or directly from the School of Metaphysics.

Thank you and sweet dreams!

Beach Ball in the Face

Do you know of anyone who actually experiences physical dreams in their sleep?

For instance, one night *I was dreaming someone was throwing a beach ball at my face and I woke up feeling it and shaking...fell asleep again and they kept throwing it at my face...each time I felt it and I woke up scared. I even "heard" it.*

What is this type of dreaming called? What is the purpose of this? What can I do to get a good night sleep as they experiences wake me up fully and it is very difficult to go back to sleep? It seems each night it is something else (a huge metal ball hitting my stomach, a letter bomb blowing up in my hand, a car hitting me in my kitchen, being punched in the face). Each time, I hear it (it seems very loud) and I FEEL it. My body jerks or reacts to the dream (punching my husband, kicking, holding my face, etc.) and then I am fully awake. At first when I "wake up" I still am stinging or hurting where I got hit.

Any advice? Any sources you could direct me to?

I appreciate your time,
M***, female

Response

Let me begin by letting you know there is nothing wrong with you. Just because most people do not share your experience does not mean you are wrong, abnormal, in need of medication or exorcism (although the latter two have been tried with some results of covering up or stopping the effects).

What is happening is you are experiencing multi-dimensional consciousness, awareness in more than the physical plane. All humans have evolved to this point by now, in other words they remember at some time having a dream, most remember a dream at least every once in a while. There are an increasing number of people worldwide who remember dreams nightly or almost nightly. And then there are the forerunners of intuitive man, like you, who experience lucid dreaming, extra-sensory awareness during the dream state. This answers your first question: What is this type of dreaming called?

Now for your second question: What is the purpose of this? The purpose is to further evolution, individually and collectively. We are, at this very instant, as individuals and as human beings evolving into a new species. This shows in our consciousness, worldwide, and it is beginning to show in our genetics. This is the purpose of your experience.

You are probably more concerned right now with the reason these dreams are happening to you, right? The reason is you have brought to yourself, to your soul, a heightened sense of awareness. You may feel alone in the experience (the sensory dreams) if the people in your life do not share such experiences, but believe me you are not alone. Many people experience the reality of subconscious mind and its intuitive abilities. You may not appreciate it now, but what you have is a built-in stimulus for learning. In other words your subconscious mind, your soul, your inner self (it is called many things by many people, that's why the School of Metaphysics exists to help educate us all so we can understand each other and our experiences better), is constantly feeding you information about your consciousness. This is beyond the physical world. It is relevant to your waking life (that's where learning the language of your dreams would be particularly helpful for you) while not being of it. This is exciting territory for the inquisitive mind, and can in time open you to worlds you presently have only an inkling of. Like so many people I've seen, you are ready to explore what is beyond the physical world. The SOM Course in Mastery of Consciousness provides a comprehensive study filled with ancient and global concepts with instruction for the means to develop your full potential as a whole self. It is taught by teachers who want to pass on to others the wisdom they have gained (they are volunteers in this endeavor, like Socrates, none of us accepts payment), and that alone makes study an enriching experience for you find there are many people like you in the world!

That's part of the answer to your last question: What can I do to get a good night's sleep as the experiences wake me up fully and it is very difficult to go back to sleep? Other answers are to consider there is a reason why you need to remember this particular dream. Begin recording the dreams, write them down. Write about them. Learn the language and interpret them placing the relevance in your waking life. Become your own teacher, rising out of the collective unconsciousness of "I'm a victim". Yes, these dreams are happening to you for a reason. Find out what it is by being a scientist about it! It's great to be in control of your own mind and your own life.

In a very practical sense, we at SOM have learned that when people begin taking this kind of control, responding to their experiences, through disciplining their attention and will power, as a secondary benefit they develop the capacity to function in more levels of consciousness. Rather than a frightening or unwanted experience, this becomes a skill that can be put to use in every area of life, from enhancing relationships with those you love to seeing connections between past choices and present situations to relieving stress and directing your health. The connection between all of these is YOU, the consciousness that makes you who you are.

MICKEY MOUSE ...
a Dream from Childhood

Hello,

I have had this reoccurring dream since I was 6 years old and I am now 19. I have always wanted help with this dream and I hope you guys can shed some light on it for me. Here it is...

I'm a little girl in a big yellow raft, going down the Grand Canyon. Mickey Mouse, Donald Duck, and I are the only ones in the raft. As we drift down the canyon, the rapids get really strong and dangerous. Then Mickey Mouse grows larger than the Grand Canyon walls. I am terrified and crying. Donald Duck and I are drowning. We are grabbing at Mickey's legs and he's shaking us off. Just as I am about to die, I always wake up.

I hope you can help me figure out what route to take in exploring my dream.

Thank you,
J***

Response

Childhood dreams often stay with us, echoes of attitudes that underlie our thinking without our ever realizing it. Understanding the dream message – even if it is years later – frees us into Self understanding and can resolve old issues that still impact us years later.

Symbolically, this dream is about forced change. Something was happening in your life that made you feel out of control. What you had been imagining was all of a sudden not going to work out or happen and it was overtaking you.

You'll want to remember what was happening in your life at age 6, when this dream came to you. It could have been a parent dying or perhaps a divorce which indeed would turn a 6-year-old's world upside down, or it could have been the action of going to school, being separated from the relatives and friends of your early years for long hours with no way to get back home. Whatever was happening, this was how you thought and felt about it, how it was affecting your consciousness.

Once determined, hopefully, you will have a different perspective on your dream, yourself, and your life. It was the memory of a dream when I too was six years old (described in **The Dreamer's Dictionary**) which spurred me to seek the meaning of dreams. I finally began finding reasonable answers when I was 22. I hope this will lead you in that direction as well.

Recurring *High School* Dream

Hi. I am actually right down the street from your Columbia Campus, and just received The Dreamer's Dictionary as a gift. I have always had peculiar dreams, but until October I didn't really search for meanings. Since than I have remembered a reoccurring dream I had throughout high school and even a couple years in middle school. I guess it occurred about once a month.

I was in my middle school, but it was full of stairs and locked doors. I couldn't find a way out. If I went to the bottom there was a river with ice chunks floating in it, but if I went up all there was, was doors. Well, I had this dream until I came to Columbia. The night of my second day of classes I had the dream, but I was able to get out. I left through the very top door that I had never noticed before. When I went in it, it was a nursery for children. There were several children there. Somehow I got out, and since I have never had the dream.

I was just wondering what it meant and what caused it to stop?

I also wondered how normal it was to remember one or multiple dreams almost ever night. I seem to remember my dreams every night unless I am sleep deprived.

Thank you for everything.

AM, female

Response

At the times you had this reoccurring dream, what you were learning was closed, limited, and you wanted it to be different, you just couldn't see how that could happen in your life. This is a common condition for teens still dependent upon parents yet becoming viable thinkers. The opportunities (doors) were always there but you didn't respond until you physically moved to Columbia.

Your conscious move to Columbia to go to school has literally opened doors in your consciousness, freeing you to learn what you've desired to learn for years. This is producing many new ideas symbolized by the children's nursery. This subconscious feedback is a positive sign that you are different now – so the same (recurring message) is no longer relevant, so the dream message changed and has since stopped.

Remembering dreams nightly means you are more conscious than most, more aware and in tune with your subconscious mind. More willing to look at yourself. Pursue it further, go beyond memory to imagined action by learning what your dreams mean and how you can become aware in the dream state.

Dracula

I keep having the same dream every night and it is really starting to creep me out.

I am walking threw a field and it starts to rain. I see a forest up ahead and decide to make camp there. As the night grows on I sit by my campfire and polish the blade on my sword. I notice a castle off in the distance that wasn't there before. All of a sudden a dark figure is standing before me. In a very deep and scary voice he says, "Behold my son you have arrived, when the day comes you will know who you are and all the truth shall be revealed." I then asked him his name and what he meant and all he said in that same voice was "I am the one you will call father and when you wake my name will appear before you." Then just as quick as he had appeared he was gone. When I awoke I looked next to my bed and a book I had never seen lay there wide open and the name Dracula was imprinted on the page.

Sincerely,
A, male

Response

Having the same dream every night means your awareness is remaining the same, so the same message is pertinent.

This dream says you are using subconscious mind to expand your awareness of relativity, the cause and effect of your life. In Eastern religions this is commonly known as karma. This has caused you to begin to realize some causes stretch beyond present time. This awareness is still unconscious in you as symbolized by the dark figure. You wonder where you came from and who you are but the answers still elude you. The information you presently have fuels your imagination of immortality.

How to respond to this dream (for when you do it will change)? The quest for immortality is older than humanity. It is the tree of life in Hebrew teachings and the tale of Gilgamesh over a thousand years before that. Immortality is the theme of the Olympian Gods and Goddesses, a theme that exists in some form in every culture, even in stories of vampires. You are ready to learn more of these, and to begin developing your consciousness in ways you probably have yet to imagine. Stretch yourself so you can KNOW. Read Leonard Orr's **Breaking the Death Habit**. It's a mind-expanding place to begin.

Found my Bracelet

Hi, I am 19 years old and I had a dream that made me so happy that I cried. Okay here it goes.... About a month ago I lost the bracelet my boyfriend gave me ($300.00 one!) anyway I was so upset. He was not happy either. Last week I went to bed thinking I would never find it.

That night I dreamed that I was sitting in my chair in my bedroom and someone was sitting on my bed and for some reason they put there hand under my mattress and pulled out my bracelet I had lost. They gave it to me and it was broke but I was happy that that person found it.

So the next morning when I woke up I thought about the dream all day. Finally I went into my room reached under my mattress and sure enough my bracelet was there. (Not broke though, I was happy about that.) I felt this weird feeling when I pulled it out. Anyway does anyone know what this could mean.
>   Thank you,
>   A***

Response

Mind is our greatest resource. It can image and accomplish anything we can imagine. It can transport us figuratively and literally to places 1000's of miles away. It can communicate our ideas to others sitting in the same room or half a world away. It can bring about inventions that transform the way people think about themselves and the world, the way they live. It can remember 20 years ago (even 200 years ago) and foresee 20 years from now.

So finding a bracelet seems completely feasible doesn't it? You can learn to access more of your mind at will – then just imagine what you may find!

Spontaneous **Combustion**

My dream involves animals.
*I was given the lead of a miniature horse to hold and
told to take care of the horse. I love horses but I'm
also a little afraid of them since I was bitten by one as
a child. The horse was white and I was very happy to
take care of it. I started to walk it along the road.
Movement in the field next to the road caught my eye.
I saw baby rabbits following their mother through the
underbrush. When I looked forward to see the mother,
she and her babies all burst into flame. Someone
asked me what had happened. I turned around to see
a man behind a counter and I noticed we were in a
big barn. I couldn't find the words to describe what I
saw. I was searching for the words "rabbit" and
"spontaneous combustion" and then the man described it for me.*

S.H.

Response
This dream is telling you your subconscious mind can
reproduce whatever your conscious mind imagines. This
is why developing conscious will (which you were doing
the day of this dream) is important to you. When you
know what you want and what you are willing to do to
achieve it your subconscious mind will go to extreme
lengths to reproduce it in your life. This is the way
desires are manifested. You might be interested in
reading a chapter from Dr. Laurel Clark's **Shaping Your
Life**, a great book on creative mind now out of print but
available on-line at www.som.org or on audio cassette
tape.

Gigantic Snakes

I was standing talking to someone (I have no clue who it was) I told him to take a look at what I was about to do. I then proceeded to run up to a snake that was sticking its head out of the ground. It was sticking out about a metre. From its diameter of about 40cm it could have been a 20metre snake. Absolutely gigantic! I ran up to the snake and stabbed it! I don't know why I did it because I'm usually petrified of snakes and would never approach them! I started running away from it because I knew that I had only hurt it and had not killed it, because I had only stabbed it with a large fork!

I was running fast and telling the person I was with to run as well. I seemed to be getting away and then I started finding what I thought to be other holes that the snake was using to move underground. It rushed through my mind that the snake would come slithering out of the holes to get me. I ran faster & faster but never felt like I was getting away. The other person was always in front of me and I was relieved about that. I don't think that I at any stage feared for my life, I just knew that I had to get away from it!

I started climbing up what looked like a wooden building that was being built. It was still very much in shell form. As I was hanging up in the building the second person (don't exactly know who it was) came to me and told me that everything was fine and that I could climb down from my perch. I asked them how he knew that everything was fine and he said to me that he had sorted out the problem. I came down to find that he had cut the head of the snake off. The body along with several other snake heads were sticking out of the hole in the ground. Even although the other snake heads were all there they seemed dead and it did not bother me, I was not alarmed!

South African Female

Response

The Dreamer's Dictionary says *snakes* symbolize

"the compulsive use of life force or creative energy. Animals in a dream including a serpent represent compulsion or habit. Throughout man's history, the snake has enjoyed a specialized symbology and therefore meaning from the Biblical serpent in the Garden of Eden to naga of Hindu teachings. The snake is even a part of the caduceus, the physician's symbol. In the Universal Language of Mind the serpent represents the compulsive use of life force or creative energy in Eastern philosophies as the Kundalini."

In your dream you are trying to kill the snake, thus you are attempting to change the way you use creative energy. This is eventually accomplished by an unknown aspect of your subconscious mind which has been with you all the time you have desired this transformation. You are at peace with the change. Confident.

This is a good example of how subconscious perspective differs from conscious perspective. If this dream happened in physical life you would have been quite bothered, but since your attention was in subconscious mind your viewpoint was not conscious, but subconscious. No fear, only acceptance and truth. That in itself is motivation to do what it takes to get closer to your own subconscious mind so you can experience those inner levels at will.

Separating *Dream* States
and *Awake* States

I recently had a dream in which a friend of mine
who is married and has a 4 year old child got
divorced because she was pregnant with a
mutual friend's baby. Throughout the dream I
kept recalling to mind real situations I've had
with her in which I asked her if all was ok, and
she would say "yeah"..but I never quite believed
her. So in the dream finding out she had had an
affair did fit in, although in reality as far as I
know she is very committed to her family.

The whole thing about the dream was that even
though I was shocked she had had an affair, my
attention was on the fact that she slept with our
mutual friend only a few days after I had visited
with him (I visited him in real life but remembered that in the dream) and during the time I
had visited I really felt if we had had more time
we may have slept together. So in the dream I
was kind of upset that she did and not me. I felt
so ugly for feeling that way when I should be
more concerned about her marriage.
S, female

Response

This dream says you have a new idea brewing that is the product of the aspects of yourself symbolized by your two friends, the woman and the man. Decipher what these people represent to you and you will have an inkling to what the idea is. This is important because the way you describe the dream says you've been suspicious of something going on but remained unconscious about it. Suspicion is different from awareness. You do sense that this aspect (the woman) is unreliable and undependable. Something happened during your day that made you admit this idea was incubating and you wanted to be a part of creating it symbolized by your desire to sleep with this mutual friend.

Possible lesson in this dream is every idea comes from you, you need only accept the truth of that and make your thoughts what you want them to be.

There are other elements here that you and others might find helpful.

As you have already figured out from your own experience and reasoning, there is a separation between our waking state of consciousness and our sleeping state of consciousness. This can be described in several ways. In a most basic sense, the waking state is meant to be a consciously aware state. Buddhism teaches about being "awake". Jesus observes that his disciples sleep, they have difficulty staying awake for even one hour with him. When we are sexually "awakened" or when someone awakens us to a new talent or skill, we have experience and our eyes are open like the Biblical woman in the

Garden of Eden. Being awake is being aware, being conscious of our experiences. When we remember dreams we bring this awakened, aware, conscious state into the inner, subconscious mind, thus beginning a journey of Self revelation that will bring enlightenment of the whole Self.

You are discovering this difference in your experience. It can, if responded to with intelligence and will, lead you to a brilliance of awareness.

The content of your dream is giving you feedback on the state of your conscious awareness. This means your subconscious mind is offering feedback about your choices, what you are thinking about and where it's coming from and will possibly lead. You have already begun distinguishing between your physical thinking and your mental thinking. This is evidenced in your comment "as far as I know she is very committed to her family" a reference to your relationship with this woman in your waking life. Paying closer attention to the origin of each thought will help to further separate your conscious thoughts and subconscious thoughts. It's like fine tuning a picture on a television screen so you can receive one station instead of two. Recording your dreams will help in this process. You will more clearly see what the dream experience is. This makes it easier to interpret the message the subconscious mind is giving you.

Both are valuable to you in their place. Until we know the value of separating the two we tend to lump all the consciousness together which leads to confusion. To become coherent is to understand the workings of our own minds in the experiences we choose.

Dating my Best Friend....

i have had this recurring dream for like 6 mos that

my best friend Mark was visiting with me from Delaware for a week. in the dream he and i were carrying on and talking like friends would. Then all of a sudden it got weird like how it would when two people fall in love. well we had started this conversation about love and how much we had felt for each other. then he looks at me and brushes my hair back and begins to kiss me. at that point i woke up but after i woke up from it i had "butterflies" in my stomach.

i swear it felt so real. i never could bring myself to tell him about it. what could this mean for me? thank you for your time,
JB, female

Response

Mark represents an aspect of your subconscious mind that you have learned how to harmonize with. Harmonization between the outer, waking conscious mind and inner, intuitive subconscious mind means both share a common ideal within your existence. This means you rely upon this aspect to fulfill your desires and it relies upon you to supply understood experiences to the soul. It's a mutually beneficial relationship that enables you to be centered, to have your head and your heart working in the same direction.

It's great to have a best friend and even greater to know what you share together is benefiting your whole self.

The Old Boyfriend

I am a college student who is living with a wonderful guy. Prior to him, was in a bad relationship with a person who I supported on my own. He is out of my life, but I never thought he would be. Early on in my current relationship, I was afraid my ex-boyfriend would come between me and my current boyfriend.

I dreamt that I was walking down a hallway at school with my backpack on my when someone grabbed me from behind and blindfolded me. I was put into the backseat of a car. I could hear the voices of two people who I recognized as my old boyfriend and his friend.

My old boyfriend was driving the car very fast. They came up on a police roadblock. They turned the car around and when down a dirt road. They put me into the trunk to hide me. They drove back to the main road and went in the opposite direction from the police block.

The whole time, the friend kept asking my old boyfriend what he thought he was doing. They still are driving very fast. I felt like I was being thrown around the trunk. They end up driving into another police roadblock. (I could somehow see this through the trunk.) The police arrested the friend without problem. My ex-boyfriend fought the police off. He hit one and kicked another. He freed himself and started running. That is when the police shot him to death.

I have had several of these dreams, where my ex-boyfriend kidnaps me, and each one ends up with him dead or hurt. These dreams seem very real and are very disturbing. Please help me make sense of this.
Thank you, S., female

Response

Dreams reflect our state of conscious awareness usually the day before you had the dream. In this dream your subconscious mind is telling you....

You are afraid because you feel your perception is blocked, that something is keeping you from seeing things as they are. This caused you to feel out of control in whatever happened during your day.

This is a repeated pattern for you that is beginning to affect your health. You know you need discipline to accomplish your goals but you remain consumed by what has happened in the past. You used to race mentally, keep your mind busy, in order to avoid the change but this didn't work today, and that's a sign of progress.

It is good that this dream disturbs you because that indicates a desire for conscious change on your part. When you're awake you want to let go of your old boyfriend who is no good for you. You need to admit that doing so means more than changing your physical actions – like not seeing him anymore. You will continue to be haunted until you are willing to come to terms mentally and emotionally. Forgiveness is the first step toward healing in these kinds of life experiences.

This dream seems to be letting you know that you have changed from being a victim. When you accept this consciously these kidnapping dreams will cease.

SHE DREAMS OF CATS
HE DREAMS HE IS LOST

*I dream of cats I used to have --they're hungry
and I can't find food or milk for them--anywhere,
and I feel helpless-if I do find food and warm
milk I'm almost about to feed them, when I wake
up.*

My husband's dream is that *he is lost --- either in
a jungle or a casino hotel or somewhere else---
but he can't find his way back.*

Thank you--E***

Response

Cats represent habits in dreams. Those are habits you used to have but no longer practice. That's probably why you wake up before feeding the cats in the dream. What you were learning the day of your dream did not apply to the old habitual ways, yet you still wanted it to. Basic message: you need to update your frame of reference in order to live in the present.

Your husband's dream indicates when he goes beyond his physical mind and body he feels out of control. The day of his dream command of his own mind was lessened. Concentration exercises would help your husband to hone his mental skills and draw upon subconscious mind purposefully without getting "lost".

Dying in Church

I am an adult who goes to church regularly. Protestant.

I dreamed that I was in a pew and some people came in late and sat down on top of me, I moved back and got stuck in between the wall and the pew. They were trying to pull me out, but I was unable to be freed and died there. I was squeezed and smothered. It was a very unpleasant dream.

What could this possibly mean?

Thanks, JM

Response

Your spiritual concepts are changing you. This change feels forced upon you, in fact restricted.

I know many Catholics who felt just this way years ago when all of a sudden many beliefs and practices were altered by the head of their church (like eating meat on Friday was all of a sudden okay and you could be divorced and marry again). Overnight, these faithful believers found the structure they'd honored overturned. Many had a hard time adjusting, some never did, leaving the religion.

It might help to think of whatever is going on in your life in a different way. Rather than your "spiritual concepts changing you" affirm "I am changing my ideas of spirituality." This will redirect your thoughts making you the center of your existence.

Furniture

Hello, I am 51 years old, and very ill. I have strange dreams and sometimes attribute them to all the medication I take.

This one was a little crazy. *I dreamed that my sister-in-law was buying furniture and none of it matched, we all wanted her to buy two couches, but my brother said she would probably just buy four chairs. She also was having new seats installed in her practically new car. She is extremely clean, and was finding half filled glasses and dishes of food under the furniture and was very upset.*

After this dream, the same night, *I dreamed that my parents (my father is deceased 9 months) moved into a different house and the front door was glass, my Dad wanted a "peephole" put in the door so he could see who might be knocking at the door. We were all trying to figure out how to install a peephole in a glass door. I suggested putting a mirror in the transom (top window) above the door.*

These were very bizarre dreams and I woke up after each of them wondering why in the world I had dreamed so. Any enlightenment?

Thanks JM St.Louis

Response

Drugs do indeed affect our perspective. Chemically altered body affects brain function which can and does interfere with the mind's capacity to communicate. Drugs often interrupt natural cycles including sleep. They can even hamper glandular function particularly actions of the hypothalamus where much of the subconscious mind's action is expressed.

These dreams are connected in message if seemingly unconnected in content. Once interpreted they do tell you about you.

Your first dream reveals what you were trying to accomplish during that day.

First is your sister-in-law. She is a conscious aspect that you need to identify. You say she is extremely clean, does this mean fastidious? Or obsessive? Or detailed? Determine her outstanding trait and you will know why your subconscious mind chose her to be in the starring role in your dream. The day of this dream, this conscious part of you was acquiring tools for mind and body cleansing. This could be anything from reading a good book on wholistic health to visiting a homeopath to attending a yoga class to praying at church. Whatever you did that day was in the direction of ridding mind and body of the old and unneeded for better functioning.

The next dream addresses how you were going about accomplishing it.

You hold ideas that you are limited, that there is only so much your superconscious mind, the divinity within you, can do. You want to please the God within and reflect it in your outer life. In fact you are very creative in your thinking about this but you continue to miss the reality that already exists.

Think of it this way, putting a peephole in a glass door is like reinventing the wheel. You need to realize you are connected to Universal Energy and this energy can heal you. You know what needs to be done, will you put your faith in it? Answering in the affirmative is how the tools you gained in the dream will be best used.

You do not mention the nature of your illness but 51 is too young to be physically impaired. Please pursue a Intuitive Health Analysis. They are invaluable in knowing what needs to be changed – and how to make those changes – for wholistic health.

43

A *Presence* in my *Dream*

Hello,

Once again I find myself turning to the School of Metaphysics for guidance and help. I attended the Springfield school for a bit in 1997. I now live in CA and the lessons that were introduced have not left my mind.

I am writing because of a dream that I had last night. I've had this dream a couple other times in the past five years. If you can offer any help it will be greatly received and appreciated.

My dream: *I feel a presence in my room, it is always a man coming to do harm. This time his face is right in mine. I lift my hand to feel if he is really there and I feel his skin. He says nothing and I immediately begin to scream for help. In the past, when I scream nothing comes out, I feel my heart will beat out of my chest because of its racing, I can't breathe.*

This time, however, I do get my scream for help out and wake myself up in the process. Oh, I am completely unable to move in the dream, which causes severe anxiety. I hear my waking self spout something similar to help but is more like, "El meee!" I turn on the lights and nothing is around.

The day of the dream I was haunted by something I did as a youngster, that obviously I have not made peace with and am wondering if this is what comes to me during these dreams? I guess I'm at the point, once again, where I am searching for answers that I won't find outside of myself.

Thank you for your help and time.

H*

Response

Good to hear from you again! You remember some important lessons from your previous study at SOM. This is reflected in the connection you make between your thoughts during the day and this dream that followed. Here are more things to consider.

This message is a thematic one reflected when you say "this time", indicating a progression from earlier dreams. This would support your idea that it is indeed connected to your progress in understanding the memory from childhood that haunts you. The dream is your subconscious mind's way of helping you do this.

The dream says you are reacting to your subconscious mind, this can happen when we don't understand the subconscious mind's duty is to fulfill conscious desires. The subconscious mind brings to us that which we image. You are getting closer to realizing this.

The progressive nature of the dream says you are taking steps toward being more responsible for what you imagine. You can help by practicing undivided attention with awareness. Be present! I hope you still have the lessons you received because you'll want to go back and study Undivided Attention and the first two lessons. They contain the keys that will unlock this dream.

Vixen *the* Vampire Slayer!

Hi,

My name is V and I came across your website after a dream I had last night. Normally I can figure out what my dreams mean myself but I am absolutely stuck on this one.

It seems to be reoccurring as well so I'm desperate to find out what it means.

In the dream I am a vampire slayer, it's set a long time ago, maybe sometime in the mid 1800's. *It is always set at night. I also sometimes work with other slayers and basically I hunt and kill vampires. I also have all these gadgets and special knives and am usually dressed in black leather. I don't really remember being scared in my dreams but I know I hate what I do but can't change the fact of what I am. I seem to always be the chosen one or something to that effect. Like I was suppose to be a slayer and have extra strength and powers for the sole purpose of killing vampires.*

The dream is always in the right order and nothing strange ever happens like flying pigs or anything like that, in fact it always seems extremely real, more than any of my other dreams. I can see everything clearly and know exactly what I'm doing and I also look different to what I do in real life.

I am just so confused as to what it all means, and I can't get over how real it seems. It is like I am actually there in someone else's body.

Please help me if you can because I can't figure it out myself.

Thank you very much for you time.

Yours sincerely

VH, Female

Response

The symbols in your dream are talking about what you are ignoring in your life. You allow many ideas to exist only in your imagination never determining their truth, never testing them in your life.

With the advent of the tv show "Buffy the Vampire Slayer" more and more young people are finding their sub-conscious mind incorporate a concept of vampire in their dreams. I say concept because the physical vampire is a bat, not a person. Books and movies stimulate our imaginations to see Dracula as a person who sucks blood.

In the Universal Language of Mind, vampires are aspects of self changed long ago that you keep resurrecting. This aspect drains other aspects. It has become the focal point of your existence. You are continuing fighting with it even though you feel powerless to change what you've done.

For you.....Realize the past is over. What you said and did are past. What you can change is your perception of what happened. The past gave you specialness. But as you say, you don't even look like you in your dream. Find a new way to be special in the now.

Another note….

Dreams are a communication from subconscious mind. Our subconscious minds have many abilities including access to the Akashic Record therefore Past Life Recall can occur in the dream state. I do not know if you are remembering a past life through the dream state, you will need to determine this. I can tell you it is more frequent than you are probably aware. In fact, I am currently writing a book on the varied abilities that are reflected in dreams. If you or anyone reading this have intuitive experiences while dreaming please e-mail us at dreams@dreamschool.org

Strange Places

Hello

In recent past I have had several dreams that are the same but different. In each of these dreams, I am in a house, or building with strange architecture, and the people in my dreams are always a combination of people I deal with now and people I use to deal with.

I am always doing strange things. For example I dreamt of an apartment that had a garage under it and my daughter and I kept going into this place to make phone calls. There was a sense that I shouldn't be there and I remember that I kept wanting to hurry before the owner of the place came home and caught us in there.

The dreams are very different. But there are key elements that make them similar. The stranger places that my dreams take place in seems to be the most memorable. More so than what and with who I am doing things. I am always in a hurry to leave, but I am filled with happiness that I got to see the people in my dreams. I also can remember waking up very amused by the lingering dream.

I hope that you can help me make sense of these dreams. I have always been aware the significance of dreams and I like to think of myself as someone who is in touch with myself. Looking at all my sides, good or bad and knowing my own limitations and potential.

Thank you.

N*

Response

People are less outstanding in your dreams at this time in your life probably because you are willing to look at yourself. The greater our willingness to express ourselves in many ways, to look for answers to questions, the more we know. Your dreams indicate what is important to you now is communicating with Universal Mind. This is our capacity to be connected with all other minds, therefore all wisdom is open to us.

You have a problem with this because you feel unworthy. This is common for people who seem to just get lucky in their intuitive abilities. They just have a knack for making people feel at home or always seeing the whole picture or knowing when something's wrong or having the right thing to say. These kind of talents that are really intuitive abilities of the subconscious mind. Look at it this way, when you study hard you know why you aced the test. When you ace it without picking up a book, you wonder how and why and not answering that can lead to self-doubt.

Since places in your dreams stand out to you this indicates that you are generally speaking more analytical, evaluating conditions, seeing the whole before the parts. Your mind tends to race so you may be heavy on the "head" side and short on "heart". Integrating your conscious and subconscious minds will help. First step? Slow the racing by learning to still your conscious mind.

Try this. Set a timer for one minute (or longer if you already practice similar disciplines). Alone, in a peaceful place, lie on your back. Inhale slowly through your nose and exhale slowly through your mouth, several times. Now set your timer. Begin counting your breaths (one inhale-exhale cycle is one) until your timer goes off. Note the number of breaths and lie there relaxed and comfortable for as long as you will. Do this simple exercise every day and then e-mail me with what's happening after two weeks.

Alice in Dream "Wonder" land

I have had this recurring dream for many years. I started having it as a child and also again as an adult. I am 32. I'd love it if you could give me some insight into what it means:

I am in a very large white room. You cannot distinguish where the walls are or even see the ceiling. There is a little house – door in the middle, a window on either side, each with a flower box. An old woman lives in the house. Next to the house, there is a huge pile of logs, shaped into a pyramid. I am walking to visit the woman when a dinosaur, like brachiosaurus, walks by and knocks over the pile of logs. The logs roll over on the house and flatten it. The old woman floats out of the house as if s........

Thank you and I look forward to your interpretation!

Leigh Anne

Response

The end of your dream got cut off in transit, but there's enough to work with here. Ideas you hold of the whole mind are being overrun by even older habits of thinking. Habits that are largely the figment of your imagination rather than rooted in fact. These are the beliefs you hold about yourself and the world. These were getting rearranged courtesy of your dinosaur, the old, outdated, no longer existing patterns of thinking.

For example, let's say you grew up not having much money to spend. Your family earned every penny and you knew where every penny was to go. This is a great asset for any reasoner and you might even appreciate what this kind of background has afforded you in understanding. However, along with the learning was disappointment from a desired toy you never got for Christmas or a too expensive prom dress or the like. This feeling is stored with all the neutral facts of the past and the good learning. Years later, you are an adult with a wonderful career, money to burn, and you still operate from the same mental picture with its feelings of "have not". In this example this is your dinosaur, no longer applicable to the present but still controlling your self-image.

It's just a hypothetical example, but look into your own thinking and find out what your dinosaur is. Change that habit and bring your ideas and feelings about them into present time.

Plane Crash

Hello

I have two dreams that are kind of strange.

Dream #1.

In the first dream, I am hugging my brother. I have not spoken with my brother in about 5 years and I don't usually dream about people I know. It is quite real and in color. I know what he is wearing and can smell his cologne. In the dream, he has gone on a plane trip with my sister and his wife. There was a plane crash and he is dead (my sister and his wife survived), though, I am hugging him and crying. He never says anything to me in the dream, and I never actually see his face. I did wake up crying, though.

Response

What is most interesting in this dream is you never see your brother, you identify him with your other senses...touch, smell. Symbolically this dream is letting you know that your affiliation with some group of people – maybe a club or church group – has caused a change in how you understand subconscious mind. You can't identify the change and are having a hard time accepting it. To better understand the dream's meaning we'd suggest identifying the aspect of yourself your brother represents. This will tell you what aspect has changed.

Dreams sometimes prompt us to physical action. Maybe it's time to see your brother again. That would be a reasonable response to this dream.

Dream #2.
This dream I just had I am in a theatre type
setting. There is a show going on (concert). I see
my husband in the audience, but I don't know
anyone else. All of a sudden I am walking
through the crowd toward the stage, singing. I
am singing a duet with another woman (I think).
The song was "Hopelessly Devoted" from
"Grease". The other person was singing the
verses, and I was singing the chorus. When the
dream ends, we are both standing on the stage
holding hands, as we sing the end of the song.
That's all I remember.

Any Ideas?
Thanks
LR, female

Response

The day of your second dream you were busy creating harmony in your life, trying to bring yourself and perhaps others together in cooperation. This would be a time to look to what happened during the day, how you were called upon to be creative perhaps in ways you never suspected you could.

This dream is a good example of how useful dream interpretation right now, today, is valuable. It helps to understand a dream anytime, even if it's a decade later. When you can understand a dream's meaning the morning you remember it, you can respond to it immediately. It's like the time difference between e-mail communication and letters by pony express. We live in an email world, let's make sure our mind development exceeds our technological ones.

Cleaning & Snakes

I am cleaning my apartment for inspection before I move out. the problem is, right after I clean it, I turn around and see that the dirt has re-appeared. the cycle continues a few more times- I clean it over again and then turn around to see that it's dirty again. the landlord shows up to inspect it, and I get nervous because it still isn't clean. but then he tells me not to worry about it and lets me go.

Then I notice that half of one of my front teeth is black. I'm able to remove the black, but throughout my dream I notice that it reappears. I keep removing it and it keeps reappearing.

There is a strange small animal like a monkey biting at my hand. I throw it to the ground, but it keeps attacking me. finally I go to the zoo and throw it into the snake cage, so that the snakes will eat it. it starts crying and calling "mama". A zookeeper then comes in and removes it from the snake cage and hands it back to me. I thought it was a small monster, but the zookeeper tells me that its a baby, and tells me its species, which I've never heard of. the reason it was biting my hand was because of compulsive teething. but it wasn't trying to attack me, it really liked me and thought I was its mother. when I looked at it again it was dead. I had thrown it around too much and the snakes had scared it so much that it died. I felt very guilty.

JM

Response

You've been reassessing your thoughts, ideas and beliefs, trying to let go but finding it difficult to do so. It's like the old saying goes, "don't sweat the small stuff". That's what you're finding when you are connected with superconscious energy. You need the tools to learn how to tell what the small stuff really is. You are aware of this.

However, you possess a habit that controls your sense of purpose. This habit is a continual thorn in your side because it often keeps you from learning. This habit was operating when you made a change that you now regret.

Sounds like you had let something go (a job, a significant other, a favorite keepsake) and later regretted it. What puts you in control of the changes in your life is imagination. For changes to be simple, easy, and even fun, use memory to see the good you've received and imagination to envision how the new will give you greater good. To earn more money, we need to leave the comfortable position, company, sometimes city behind. We must make space for the new. Sounds like you wanted to do this but faltered when you saw the effort it would require to move through the change.

Now is the time to keep your sights on where you are going.

Dreaming of my
recently deceased Mother
.... Communication?

Hello,
My Mother died almost 2 months ago. Two nights
before she died,

*I dreamed that I was lying in the family room with
her (which I was) and saw her moving back and
forth across the room, not walking but simply
moving back and forth. The look on her face was
somewhat serious – as though she had an agenda.*

*Two weeks later (after she died) I had a dream in
which she called me. She told me that she was going
to see the Apostle. I asked her if I could call her
sometime and she said yes. I wrote down notes and
brought them into a house to tell my dad, but my
notes faded and the telephone number barely
remained legible, but I could still read it.*

Last night I had a third dream. *This time I dreamed
that I was with my Mother just before she died. I
was just talking with her and she was in a lot of*

*pain (she died of cancer). We talked for a while and
I got her something to drink (Pepsi). (background:
The day before she died, I had asked her if we could
have a day of just the family so that we could visit
more one-on-one since she had tons of friends
always coming by – she said yes we'd have a "family day" – however she died that night). In the
dream, we then hugged each other for a while and
she told me how proud she was of me and how
much I meant to her. I have been longing to hug my
Mother since she died. During the dream, I knew
that the hug was very special because somehow I
knew she was not alive outside of my dream -
apparently I knew I was dreaming within my dream.*

I then woke up.

Additionally, for some reason I felt I was going to dream
about my Mom that night. I was not overly surprised to
have a dream of her that night. Could I be communicating with my Mom in all 3 dreams? I would like to hear
your assessments. Thank you.
MDL, female age 32

Response

There are several different dream experiences to address here. First, your dream before your mother died was from the sound of it an actual inner level experience. You were watching her move beyond the physical into the etheric plane.

Second, the dream two weeks later was a message from you about you. The way you understand your own divinity had changed. Although what your superconscious mind gives you remained the same, the way it receives has changed in your mind. This type of attitude change concerning your own authority is a natural part of no longer having a parent with you. It is a stimulus for greater growth and learning when we embrace it as such.

Third dream reveals what has changed and how it came about. Through your waking experience of your mother leaving her physical body you learned something about eternal life - that you exist with or without the outer shell. This is what changed. How it changed was through forgiveness. The fact that you knew you were dreaming while in the dream says this was a lucid dream.

Here you have several examples of subconscious experience. First, the inner level experience where you did communicate apart from the body with another. Second, dream message about the state of your conscious awareness. Third, lucid dream. I understand it was important to you to believe you communicated with your mother following her withdrawal from physical life, but in truth the dream messages you received will be more meaningful for you in the days and years ahead for they speak to your willingness to be transformed by your experience and that's the reason we are here in the material plane.

A Lingering Dream...

I'm hoping you can interpret a dream I had several weeks ago but that has lingered in my mind:

My father (who has been dead for 17 years) was the center of focus. I was under the nook of one arm and a small child (maybe 1-2 ish) was under the other arm. There are no words spoken but it is known that the child is dying.

This has bothered me since I dreamt it. Any ideas on interpretation??? I'd appreciate it.

Thanks.
KD in Cleveland

Response

This dream reflects a loss of innocence. As we learn more (no matter what our age) and develop we gain opportunities to experience and understand on a greater level. When we embrace these we experience greater light of awareness, more compassion and understanding. When we want things to remain the same this can lead to regret. Regret is behind the loss of innocence.

This dream is talking about your feeling that you are going to lose a new idea that was precious to you. What I will say to you is hold onto your dreams. Because you are a creative being you can cause your idea to mature and flourish. If you give it up, it will be your choice alone and not a function of someone or something else forcing you to sacrifice. This idea is important to you, represented by the presence of your father. Find a way to nurture it to maturity.

Scorpions

I wake up in my bedroom in the middle of the night. my 2 dogs are lying on the floor. its very dark in my room. my dogs look scared. I see that there are small black scorpions crawling all over my room. they start crawling onto me. at first I'm frightened, but then a voice inside me tells me that as long as I don't fear them, they will not sting me.

so I change my view of them from being dangerous scorpions to being small cute bugs, so I'm no longer afraid of them. I walk around with them attached to me for awhile, but then I decide I need to go back to bed. I pull each one off of me and set them on a table. I accidentally injure the first one I pull off, not realizing it is so fragile. after I pull them off me and put them down, they hardly move. they lay on their backs like all of their energy has been drained. then a storm breaks out outside.

I call Nancy (a spiritual woman I know). she gives me the number of a woman to call. I go to call this woman, who I do not know. I feel awkward calling her because I don't think she knows who I am, and I don't know what I even want to ask her. when she answers I introduce myself and she replies, "oh, I've been waiting to hear from you!" then she tells me what seems to be information about my future.

I suddenly saw myself standing in the middle of a freeway surrounded by speeding vehicles. she tells me, "you will walk down the middle of the road. do not worry about the speeding cars. they cant hit you." so I start to walk and I notice that the cars go around me.

JM, 21 fem

Response

You have a familiar way of thinking which keeps you in ignorance. It could be a way of pretending things are different than they are or seeing only what you want to see or even lying to yourself. Whatever it is, it's a habit. And you have other more serious habits that you think you can control but you can't. This leads to turmoil in your life.

You rely on a conscious aspect (symbolized by Nancy) to help you when you get yourself in trouble like this. This aspect is helping you become aware of an unconscious part of yourself that is aware of goals you yourself may have forgotten or ignored.

An example of this type of consciousness might be....You want to quit smoking. You think you can be around others who smoke, but you find when you're with them you smoke "just one". This then feeds the old habit which leads to the turmoil. The Nancy part of you believes you can beat this because smoking is not in alignment with your ideas of being spiritual. She is helping you learn how to keep your ideals holy through the aspect of the unfamiliar woman. As you practice will power and determination this woman will begin appearing in your dreams as someone you know in your life who exhibits these qualities.

Your dream message ends by letting you know you are reminded of your goal and the path to reach it but you are not yet committed to getting there. Keep moving on it and you will reach your goal.

Shot in the *Back*

I recently had a dream where

I was in my old high school's office. A girl walked in and asked me if it was hilltop high and I looked up at the large sign which read" hilltop high" and answered her "yes". I recall that the instant she walked in I knew that there would be trouble.

As soon as she asked me if this was the high school, she pulled out a gun and shot me point blank in the back. I fell to the ground with the strangest most sensational feeling of my life being drawn right out of me. It was as though a glass of water was slowly being poured out.

Anyway, I remember saying to myself that I must not close my eyes and let go of life. I was thinking that as long as I remained conscious I wouldn't die. I also remember that I had to appear to be dead by slightly closing my eyes so that the girl would leave having accomplished her goal. Then lying there, I remember fighting to stay alive and refusing the drowsy confusion. I also was trying to hang on by telling myself that the wound was inflicted low and beneath my heart more near my kidney and that I could survive this. I was waiting for her to scurry away so I could yell out for my husband's name

and then I woke up frightened.
T, 30 yr old female

Response

This nightmare revolves around previous ways of learning, ways that no longer apply but are influencing you toward changes you have no intention of making. The girl with the gun is an aspect of yourself that you know causes you "trouble". Yet you have allowed this aspect to exist, to interfere with your learning, and to force itself upon you and others. Rather than give in to this part of yourself you cause yourself to "look", seeking to perceive things differently than before.

Two particularly significant bits of information come late in the dream. First the dream-fact that you pretend to be dead so the girl can accomplish her goal. This may well be telling you how you let this aspect have so much control in your life...that you pretend in order to avoid change. This leads to the second piece which is the placement of the wound. The change is not in understanding, but in feeling guilty. Those are the pieces, they sound most revealing, if you need more help please let us know.

THE *ELEVATOR DREAMS*

I am 33 years old and have been working in the same building for the past 11 years.

I have this recurring dream about being in the building and taking an elevator up to my office. Sometimes the elevator makes it to my floor but the hallways always look different. In other dreams the elevator opens to what I think is my floor but the offices are different or there is a sewing room with women sitting around machines making clothes. If I am not going to make it to an office floor, the elevator car begins to shake from side to side, like it is on a loose cable and then drops. Sometimes there are co-workers on the elevator with me and other times it is strangers in the building. There have been times when I stepped on the elevator car and noticed it was moving around and got off because I knew it was going to fall.

I have this dream quite regularly, at least once a month and cannot for the life of me understand what I am dreaming about. Any help you can offer would be greatly appreciated!

Sincerely
ML, female

Response

The way you are producing in your life is opening the way you can use subconscious mind, but you're unsure what to do when you get there. It's like doing the right thing then becoming more open to others because of it and finding yourself suddenly reading other people's minds! Or maybe you've been doing your best so you're getting all of these offers to work for others, and when you take *the* job you're suddenly insecure about your qualifications. These insecurities arise when you become concerned with how you appear to others. This is a distraction away from who you are and what you know.

Some days you are able to draw on subconscious mind but fear brings attention back to the physical world.

With these kinds of dreams, especially recurring in your life, it sounds like you are ready for the course in metaphysics taught through the School of Metaphysics. This course is offered through correspondence study. It teaches the disciplines you are seeking, disciplines that enable you to scientifically experience conscious, subconscious, and superconscious mind with awareness.

"TOY STORY" PIG

I rarely remember my dreams, but woke up in the middle of this one.

I was getting ready to get on the Space Shuttle, but I couldn't go until I shaved a pig (especially its feet). The pig resembled the pig in Toy Story, but would be about 4 feet high standing up. It was covered with straight black hair like you might find on a dog.

I really don't know where this came from.
38, Male Cleveland, OH USA

Response
Sometimes our dreams are outrageous to get our attention. By your reaction, this one seems to be one of those.

Symbolically speaking the dream says you want to find others with which to explore the inner realms of existence but you are distracted by a way you use your imagination (maybe you think you already know too much, or too little? Or maybe you're a prisoner of the I'll-figure-it-out-myself), compulsively. Find out what the habit is and you'll know what's keeping you from achieving your goal.

DREAMING ABOUT *BLOOD*

*My two granddaughters, 15 and 13, both, on
different nights, one didn't know about the other's
dream, dreamed about blood, they were bleeding as
their period, then it was like a river.*
 Does anyone know what the dream means? I would
really appreciate any answers you would have on
this.
Thank you very much.

Response

Blood represents life force in the Universal Language of
Mind. These dreams are highly symbolic and reminis-
cent of many classical holy scriptures. If you are familiar
with the Bible you can see the imagery in several
contexts.

For your adolescent granddaughters they do not
signify ill health, rather they are representative of the
natural changes in energy associated with puberty. Puberty is the time of physical development when the
Kundalini, the creative energy, awakens and becomes
active. The "river" means the supply of creative energy
is endless.

To help your grandchildren, talk to them about
their hopes and dreams. Help them fashion ideals and
goals from these. Then empower them by giving them
the tools for creating what they want. This will give this
energy a direction and your granddaughters self-esteem
and self-confidence.

For more on kundalini you might want to read my
book titled **Kundalini Rising: Mastering Creative
Energies**, then begin taking the SOM course.

GRAMPA, THE TEDDY BEAR, AND THE STAIRS

When I was little I had this reoccurring dream every month or so. *My grandfather, who passed away in 1991, would stand at the top of the staircase in my house. He would throw my stuffed teddy bear down the stairs, and I would run down to get it and bring it back up to him, only to have him throw it down again. This would continue like a game of fetch throughout the entire dream. When my grampa passed away I stopped having the dream......*

I've always wondered what this dream meant, can you help me??

J*, female, NY

Response

Symbolically the dream reflects the rapport you had with Superconscious mind. Moving your attention out into the physical world and going back to superconscious mind. We have this kind of mobility in mind when young and tend to lose it as we trade inner awareness for outer peer acceptance and pressure. If this rapport has been lost it can be restored through daily meditation and learning to live meditatively.

J*, it is entirely possible that this was your way of "playing" with your granddad in the inner levels when you were young. Particularly if you didn't have much opportunity to interact physically. This inner level rapport is entirely possible.

RECURRING DREAMS ABOUT
SEXUAL ENCOUNTERS

It seems I have reoccurring dreams about different men and having sexual encounters with them. Some of the men I have had relationships with in the past and others I don't know at all. I like the experience. It is not "bad" in my dreams. I feel deeply for these people in my dreams.

I am married with two children and am 38 years old. I don't feel guilty about the dreams when I wake up like I used to. Now I am willing to search for the meaning, instead of berating myself and thinking I am a total cheat!

Response

Good for you! Dreams originate not from physical thinking but subconscious thinking. They are in symbols reflecting subconscious mind's perception of the state of conscious awareness. They are like a report card or diagnostic report.

This report indicates harmony between you and many subconscious aspects. You are calling upon many parts of your subconscious mind to fulfill your desires. Sexual dreams tell us that conscious and subconscious minds are working together toward the same objective.

GETTING SEPARATED FROM OTHERS

I write to you on my mother's behalf. She recently told me of a recurring dream she has been having since her mother died in October. She said the people change and the places change, but the consistent part of the dream is that she is with a group of people and somehow gets separated from them. She can't find her way back to where she is suppose to be. She equates it to being in a maze, and no matter how hard she tries, she cannot get back to her friends. She is left all alone and trying to remember how to get back to where she started.

Any help would be appreciated.

Response

When we dream we are lost this indicates a need to live in the present – to be here now. It is significant this dream started after your mother's mother died. Perhaps your mother tended to her needs during her last days and since has had difficulty adjusting to her freedom of time. Or maybe they were best friends and your mom has yet to let go and learn to live.

Whichever, you can help your mom by bringing her attention to here and now. Do something together – take a class, pursue a hobby, set up regular visits or outings or phone calls. These will help give her something in the present to look forward to and do. Encourage her to make new friends and set goals. Love her and let her know you love her every day. Some way.

CHEATING ON SPOUSE

My husband often dreams that I have, or am, cheating on him. These are almost the only dreams that he ever remembers. I keep trying to tell him that his dreams are not telling him that I am cheating, have cheated or will cheat, but that they are telling him something about himself. Can you please tell me what exactly these dreams are telling him about himself?

Response

These dreams mean that he believes his subconscious mind does not fulfill his desires.

Research has shown that many people who dream that their spouse is unfaithful do harbor thoughts, fears, about this during their waking hours. If this is the case, your husband would do well to begin giving more, living up to being the husband he wants to be, for in so doing he will better serve himself and definitely improve his marriage.

SEVERAL DREAMS
ABOUT THE *BRONX*

I am very interested in finding out more about several dreams I have had in the past few weeks. I live in New York and was born in the Bronx.

In my first dream several weeks ago,

I was back in my room in my mom and dad's house (both parents are deceased) and I opened the bedroom door to find a pool of water in the hallway. In the water was 4 frogs and two white snakes. I called for my father and he came running with a rake but the water was dark and he could not reach the frogs or snakes. He told me to go back in my room and everything would be all right. Soon after, I opened the door again and my mom was near her bedroom door. I told her to watch out for the snakes and she grabbed one and the snake was now black. She squeezed it and said don't worry it will be all right now. I then awoke.

My next dream a few weeks later was that *I was in my bedroom at home and a window was opened and the wind was blowing. I proceeded down the hallway which was full of hanging plants and spraying water. When I got to the end of the hallway, I saw several people dressed in black with their backs to me. I was very frightened and ran through them yelling that they can't have me. Soon after I was in my friend's bedroom and the door squeaked and opened. I saw someone with a hooded mask and a very frightening face. I woke up from the dream screaming.*

Several days later, *I dreamt that a man was passing over my bed with a plaid jacket and dark hair. He passed over several times and again I awoke screaming.*

My mom died 7 years ago and the might before she died I had a dream that I feel is of importance. My mom dying and could not speak at the time. I was sleeping in the bed next to her. My sister woke me and said I was moaning. The dream was:

I saw my mom get out of the bed from where she was dying and she was dressed so beautifully, she said I'm going up stairs soon and I love you all very much. I woke up after my sister woke, me.

My mom died the next day. If possible, could you interpret any of these dreams and let me know. Thanks.
Caroline

Response

These dreams do seem progressive, offering insight into something that has been buried unconsciously and now is becoming conscious.

Dream 1 reflects a memory of your experiences with superconscious mind earlier in your life and how this memory has affected your conscious life. You have been habitual with your creativity and so wisdom from your life experiences has remained unconscious. There is much more that you are capable of than you have displayed.

Dream 2 is a nightmare because you are out of control. There are parts of you, both inner and outer, that are interfering with how you use your mind to get what you want. They do not express honesty. The problem, and probably the unconscious habit, is keeping secrets.

Dream 3 indicates you were afraid of assimilating, thinking and analyzing, what you were learning and so you felt forced to face it.

These three dreams are connected and reveal something surfacing in your life that, when given attention, could change how you understand your ability to create what you desire. It is worth exploring.

The last dream about your mother indicates your realization that superconsciousness is separate from the rest of mind. This is a natural evolvement of thinking during this kind of life experience. Attending a parent's release from the physical world, puts us in contact with our own sense of death and immortality.

FEET

I dream almost every night and lately I've noticed that in a lot of the dreams I have bare feet. I know that this symbolizes truth & honesty; however, I have one more twist to it all. I have tattoos on my ankles and one on my toe that I am always trying to keep my dad from seeing them.
thanks for your help.
j., female, tx

Response
Feet symbolize our spiritual foundation. **The Dreamer's Dictionary** says, "This foundation is the combination of the permanent understandings of creation previously gained and held in the soul plus the present conscious attitudes that will foster and enrich spiritual progression. Feet in a dream will tend to indicate the dreamer's place of security."

What is worthy of noting in your dreams is the desire to hide your tattooed ankles from your dad. This means your spiritual foundation is not in alignment with Superconscious Mind. What does that mean? It could be false beliefs, which means the honesty part needs some investigation on your part. Maybe it's time for your beliefs about spirituality to be reviewed and updated.

Given a Mission

I am in my backyard, and a friend tells me that I need to dig three holes in the ground and place an item in each hole. (I cant remember what the items were). when each item was thrown into the hole, it transformed into something else. (again, I cant remember what they became).

Then I was in a building, on a second floor landing. there was a young man in there trying to kill an older man who was very obese. he shot the man, but he didn't die. so then he cut him with a blade, almost cutting him in half, but he still wouldn't die.

The man was now naked and horribly bleeding, and trying to run away. he was telling the man who was trying to murder him that he wasn't going to let him take his life. the assailant shot at him again, and killed him.

Then someone gave me a name and phone number I needed to call. the name read "malicha". It was a girl. I was given a mission. I needed to help her save her father, who was about to die by being consumed by fire. I needed to warn her, and give her advice on how to save him. I made three attempts to call her, and each time her father answered, and then handed the phone to her. I tried to warn her that her father was about to die, but I didn't know how to tell her, and I had no solution for her.

Before calling her the third time, I looked at my bead bracelet, and the beads began to look like small orbs of fire. it was a sign of urgency, that I needed to do something immediately. I called a third time. this time the father said, "ok, you can talk to her...but this is the last time you can call here." when she got on the phone,

I told her that her father was about to be consumed by fire, and the only way she could stop it was for her to go into the water.

Then we hung up, and I felt good, like I'd accomplished something. then a white truck drove by me, and Christ Jesus jumped out of it and ran up and hugged me and I felt very happy.

J.M., 21 yr. fem. from CA

Response

What a great learning day you must have had!

Subconscious mind is like a garden where we plants seeds and with care in time our garden flourishes. This dream reflects what you were learning about your own capacity for seed ideas that become your physical life.

You have been planting seed ideas that are not strong enough to maintain integrity. Since your ideas are weak the subconscious mind cannot fulfill your desires, they "die out" long before they would manifest. They are like seeds that have barely sprouted or a fetus in a womb.

When you aren't getting what you want an unfamiliar conscious aspect kicks in giving you the decisiveness you see yourself as lacking. You are unaware of your connection to superconsciousness but it is there.

What became apparent is your need to cooperate with your own desires. Cooperation causes your ideas to grow, to move through the inner levels of consciousness (there are four distinct ones). This helps you become more conscious of your divinity, your superconsciousness.

A SON DIES

On Mother's Day eve *I dreamed that my youngest son, age 7, had died. I seem to remember that the cause was at first unknown. The weirdest thing was that we had invited some of his friends to a party/funeral!*

I should tell you that he has recently been complaining about headaches, although the doctor says he's OK. Also, I had a daughter that died at age 10 of a brain tumor. Am I just scared of the same thing?

Response

It is possible you are scared of losing a child, that would not be irrational fear although certainly one you'd rather be free of. What I can tell you is that an Intuitive Health Analysis on your son is in order. They go a long way in easing a parent's mind because they identify the condition mentally, emotionally and physically plus give suggestions for child and parent. More from a parent's perspective can be found in the book **First Opinion: Wholistic Health Care for the 21st Century** on page 99.

As for your dream, it indicates that a new subconscious idea (symbolized by your son) has changed and that this has affected other ideas. Whatever your son represents to you, whatever you see as his outstanding characteristic, that is the part of you he represents. Determine that and you will have a clue to the nature of the idea that has changed.

GIRLFRIEND

I recently had a dream concerning my girlfriend.
We recently had a discussion about us and where
our relationship was heading. The following
night *I had a dream in which I was trying to find
her, but was unable to locate her. I was checking
all over the house I grew up in as a child. I kept
searching the same rooms over and over and was
unable to find her. The rooms in my dream were
exactly how they were when I was growing up. I
can't understand why I was looking in the house I
grew up in and why I was terrified when I
couldn't locate her.*

Any help would be appreciated.
DL, male

Response

DL, each dream is all about you, and all the people and things
within the dream represent all parts of you. This dream says
you are becoming aware of how empty you would feel
without the presence of your inner self; you feel childlike in
how you think and feel, and this generates more emotions.

You seem puzzled by the dream setting being your
childhood house. This shows that you are feeling lost in a
familiar place in mind associated with the lesser experienced
you. Rather than using immature thoughts and attitudes, use
all the mind you have developed, as an adult: Here, you will
find the presence of your inner self when you ask questions
and listen intently to within.

Your current relationship with your subconscious mind
will not be found in the past, you must create it in the now.

PREMONITIONS
BY DAY AND NIGHT

For about a year now I have been experiencing
what could be called "premonitions" except that
what happens is I will think or talk about something or someone and it will happen or the person
will call or show up. For instance, talking or
thinking about a song and it will come on the T.V.
or radio. At first I thought it was a coincidence
(even though I don't really believe in them) but it
has happened too many times and very often, and
just recently it happened in a dream, I dreamed
about a contest I had won 2 weeks prior and the
prize showed up in the mail that next morning.
So my uncle advised me to write you. Thank you.
Hoping for insight....

HP, female

Response

When scientists study premonition they call it mathematical probability. Premonition, the knowing of the occurrence of something before it physically occurs, is a very real function of subconscious mind. Each of us can be scientists, using our own lives as our laboratories, learning to ascertain the truth of our own existence. This is part of practical metaphysics. The kind of metaphysics that brings answers to universal questions while solving the problems of our day.

All minds are connected through what is termed Universal Mind. This enables movement of thought to and from each of us. Each of us are both sending and receiving stations. Those who are more closely linked to soul are more aware than those who are not. Suggestions for development and use of your ability include logging your experiences (the scientific approach), recording evidence of when the inklings you experience do lead to physical events and when they do not. You will also need to factor in free will. For instance if you perceive your friend Mark will call you around dinner and he doesn't call until an hour after dinner it could be because he was later getting home or his roommate was tying up the line on the Internet!

You can build your ability while testing it by setting up intentional experiments with friends. Students in School of Metaphysics classes do this in a variety ways as part of their study and development. Agreed upon a time of day when you will project a thought to your friend. He or she will be attentive to you at that time, becoming aware of whatever enters his/her mind. Then fifteen minutes later you receive your friend's projected thought. Compare notes. You'll be surprised over a several month period of time what you discover about the power of your mind.

81

READY TO STUDY...AGAIN

I was a member of SOM Berwyn, Illinois in 1988 - 1990. By attending, I learned many things. I was able to produce premonitory dreams. The most significant of these dreams included the death of my husband. I discontinued my studies after he died tragically.

I thought, "what a tremendous burden, to know the fate of someone that I love." From then on, I chose to block out any and all knowing. I repressed my abilities for nearly 7 years and over the last 4 little by little it is coming back. I think I am at a point in my life where I would cherish being around others like me.

I now live in Indiana and I would like to come back to SOM.
Please respond......
Thanks
EWM

Response

Welcome! Your life must have unfolded in many ways since your studied a dozen years ago. I can only imagine why you would have abandoned your study at a moment in your life when you perhaps needed it the most. Whatever human emotions propelled you to that end I am glad you now can make the space in your life to move toward answering lingering questions. How difficult these years must have been for you. And how necessary to lead you to this point.

The greatest challenges in our lives revolve around what we do not understand. Each of us has every available opportunity for a positive existence if we will only choose it. Just the act of setting our sights on understanding our experience elevates our consciousness. We can perceive more. We can give more. We can feel more. Choosing otherwise deems the not understood experiences in our lives a tragedy. I hope your choices now will lead you beyond acceptance and reconciliation to the compassion that unites soul.

The question becomes where do you want to begin? Since you studied at SOM every part of our School has evolved. In 2001, the entire course is new, reflecting thirty years of development in consciousness. We call them the Millennial Lessons. The nearest city (to you) where these are taught would either be Chicago or Indianapolis. If these are not within driving distance and you do not want to relocate to go to school, the First Level of the course is taught through correspondence with a teacher at the College of Metaphysics.

We now have this website devoted to dreams. **The Dreamer's Dictionary** includes 1000's of dream symbols interpreted in the Universal Language of Mind. **The Bible Interpreted in Dream Symbols** is exactly what it says, an awesome book written by four authors over 25 years. For a complete listing of our books, many of which are no longer in print but are online at SOM's virtual library at www.som.org.

In addition to the community services you probably remember from your earlier days of study at SOM, we now offer explorations called Spiritual Renaissance Weekends on our College campus. These include Intuitive Reports designed for and offered only during these weekends. We still offer Past Life explorations and Intuitive Health Analyses for people from around the world. Arrangements can be made through the mail.

We look forward to hearing from you soon.

MORE DREAMS THAT COME TRUE..
...this time a child's

Dear sir,
I just heard about you from searching on internet, and
I thought you might help us clear our heads about a
little worry we have. There is a 8 years old boy, a
son of my cousin, who is dreaming some things that
quite a few days later are becoming true.

The first time he saw a dream about a lottery,
and asked his mom to buy him lottery tickets from
Red Cross as he dreamed, and instead of a change the
seller gave them one more ticket from other lottery,
which it results to be a winning one. Next time he
dreamed about a place burning in a center of our
town, and told his mother his dream in a morning. A
few days later that dream became true, in fact in our
city was burned one of the main cultural building just
like the boy described it.

I should ask for excuse for my bad English, but
I hope it will not be a problem. If you have any
counsel for us, what should we do with the boy and
how could we respond to his "talent", please do not
hesitate to email us.

Sincerely yours
LB and VK

Response

Dreams, at any age, are the means for the subconscious mind to communicate with the waking, conscious mind. This is true for the people above who have e-mailed us and for this eight year old boy. His dreams have a dual function: a personal message for the boy about the boy and a look at probable future events. What is most important is the guidance you, and the boy's parents can offer him. The attitudes of the adults around him will shape his attitude toward his dreams and his abilities. By seeking education on dreams, you are to be highly commended, for as you learn you have knowledge and wisdom to offer rather than superstition and fear.

These are the steps to take. First begin to be a student of dreams yourselves. Record your dreams and encourage the boy to record his. Bring an attitude of scientific discovery and research to your experiences and his. This will give both of you a needed sense of being in control of what is occurring.

Next begin to study and learn the Universal Language of Mind. Reference the Nine Steps to Dreaming and begin using them. The boy will imitate what he sees you do. Children learn what they live. Telling him to do something pales in the presence of just one adult who has experience and wisdom.

A good book to read about the capacity of the mind is Dr. Daniel Condron's **Superconscious Meditation**. Any of the vast material available at this website and at www.som.org will answer some of your questions and be of help concerning the nature of precognitive dreams. Personal contact is always recommended and you can pursue correspondence with a teacher at our headquarters or write or call us with questions.

A book is now being written which we hope to publish this year concerning the way the varied capacities in subconscious mind make themselves known during our sleeping time through what we remember as dreams. What is most important is to let the boy know his "special" ability is supernormal, an ability more and more people are beginning to exhibit. Encourage him to tell his dreams upon awakening, writing them down, and interpreting their meaning. Then going back to log those that "come true".

The two dreams you cite have a distinct message for the boy. The first says he is receiving value from the experiences that are aligned with his Superconscious Mind, his purpose for existence. A strong spiritual foundation is important for this boy to build. In the second dream his subconscious mind was telling him whatever he had experienced during the day had caused an expansion in his way of thinking that he felt was beyond his control. When parents are in touch with their child's daily experiences, dreams can be a wonderful educational tool to help that child grow and mature as a thinking, compassionate person. Dreams always tell the truth about our state of awareness.

Concerning the precognitive nature of these dreams, explain to the boy that every person has free will, the freedom to choose how he or she will think. He will determine with your help whether he sees this ability as an asset or a curse (see e-mail above). When the dream is about the boy he can decide on a different course of action as you discuss his dreams if this new course is deemed more beneficial. If the dream is about something separate from the boy, like the burning building, this is where the scientific investigation will bring great results. The science will give you and the boy the power to discern his precognitive dreams and his non-precognitive dreams. This then will be invaluable in determining if and when to act upon the dream so the probable outcome changes.

People have dreamed of all sorts of tragedies, plane crashes, houses burning, people dying. Some react to their dreams sometimes shutting down dream recall altogether, others learn to use the dreams to prepare themselves and others for what might happen, still others respond to them by changing the course of history. Which do you want for this eight year old boy?

Let us know when and how we can assist.

Confusing Dreams

I am writing in hopes of gaining some insight into my dream life and the possibility that I could have some intuitive abilities. I learned of the School of Metaphysics from my uncle who attended a few years back.

I've always had the ability to remember my dreams with no need to write them down. I've always analyzed my dreams with the use of dream dictionaries and my own intuition and been pretty successful, until I was 17 and was left paralyzed from a traumatic car accident. Since then my dream life has become extremely active, having many dreams each night and remembering all of the most dominant and/or most recent (before I awake) and parts of the rest makes them very difficult to interpret.

It's extremely hard to tell which dream I had which day and to tell which part belongs to which dream...it's very confusing, and since I remember them for up to 2 weeks sometimes, it makes it even worse. So I haven't been able to interpret my dreams very well for quite a while.

HP, female

Response
It is very common, when the body is impaired in some way, for the mind to seem more active. It is as if the mind becomes more active now that the body is not. Many people we have spoken with in similar conditions to yours say their dream life has become more real. Some would discount this as wish fulfillment or an escape on the part of a person whose body has seemingly turned against them. Our research shows an entirely different point of view.

88

You have always found value in your dreams, so you have given attention to the inner workings of your own mind. Now, more than ever, you are investigating the fascinating world that exists beyond the physical plane. The reality of dreams, where you can leave the limits of the physical world, is brought home to any serious student of this night time world. The inner worlds exist as assuredly as this physical world of matter, and owing to the nature of intelligence and free will we can experience in those worlds. Thus it is common for an average person to become exceptional in dreams, or a homely person to become handsomely beautiful, or a paraplegic to run and dance. You can fulfill many desires in these inner worlds while you find answers and meaning in the messages they convey.

Since your command of will has yet to match the quickening of the recall of dreams I would suggest recording your dreams on audio cassette. There are many ways to accomplish this which you are probably far more familiar with than I. If for some reason this is not possible, as a friend or loved one to write them for you. Directing your thoughts to retain the details of the dreams will strengthen your will, and therefore your memory. This is the kind of practice our students undertake to gain mind mastery. Your desire to remember and understand your dreams may well be the motivation to improve your mental capabilities. I encourage you to study metaphysics, for in fact, what you learn can aid in your recovery and your healing while answering many questions. We have met some remarkable people with remarkable stories...check out *Colonel Whitten's Nephew's* story at www.som.org .

Crow Flying by her Car

Here it goes.

I was driving down the road. The roof of my car was gone, all of the windows were down. There was a HUGE crow flying level with my head. No matter what speed I drove, the crow stayed. I couldn't roll up the window and was scared. The crow never did anything it just flew right along beside the car. I woke up and that was it.

IL, Female

Response

Birds in a dream represent compulsive thoughts in subconscious mind. This symbol is paired with driving down the road which represents your direction in life. Your direction is determined by the goals and ideals you have made your own. In this dream your physical actions are moving toward your goal but they are wearing on your body. There is every indication you are relying upon your inner, subconscious mind to pick up the slack of your racing through life. The biggest message here is you are taking your subconscious mind for granted. Get to know this part of yourself. Make an effort to record all your dreams, not just the ones that frighten or shock you. Be willing to attend that inner voice of conscience. It is often the wisdom of subconscious mind.

Another suggestion for appreciating your subconscious self.....Do you exhibit a talent that no one taught you during this lifetime? Be attentive to this talent, cultivate it, so it becomes a part of your conscious awareness. Be more willing to use your talents to bring deeper understanding to your soul. This will mean more to you than accomplishing a hundred physical goals.

Dream of *Richard Nixon*

I was having sex with my boyfriend outside in what
seemed like a big pipe and we saw someone coming. I
started to run away and try to hide. When I went to go
see who it was it was Richard Nixon. I was still ducking
and trying to hide from him while my boyfriend was
talking to Nixon totally naked. Then Nixon dipped his
head in a pool and left. The last thing I remember is my
boyfriend saying, "That was the most embarrassing
thing ever."
Then I woke up. Please tell me what that was all about!
SC, Female

Response

There are two key elements in this dream: sex symbolizing
harmony between conscious and subconscious minds for the
purpose of creation, and Nixon (we assume you are referring
to the former U.S. president) who represents a superconscious
aspect of self. The openness between your inner and outer
selves has produced awareness in your conscious mind.
During your day's experience, your conscious and subconscious minds were working together which aligned with
Superconscious mind causing a new awareness in your conscious mind. This probably came in the act of fulfilling a
desire that brought a sense of peace. Whether this manifested
as a new realization of truth about Self and others or a
reconciliation in Self with others or just a feeling of profound
gratitude, the experience went all the way through you, and
you need to receive its power.

There is some indication that you did not do this the day
you had this dream. This could be tied to your subconscious
mind's choice of a president (it could have been Lincoln or
Kennedy). Something to ask yourself and figure out is why
Nixon, what is unique about him that your subconscious mind
chose him to convey the message?

91

Distractions...*on the way to the Store*

Thank you for the interpretation of the dream I sent you. It was very enlightening. Here is another one I had around the same time.

I was in a pickup truck driving to a shopping plaza (stores all in a row). I entered on one end of the plaza and was driving slowly to the other end. My goal was to go to Kohls which was beyond the plaza. As I began my drive past the stores, there was a crowd of teenagers hanging around outside. They were a nuisance. One of them walked out in front of me and I had to brake. I went on and the crowd lessened. I was almost at the end when a lady with a walker appeared at the curb. She was going to cross the street but I was in a hurry and didn't see her until I had passed her. I felt guilty that I did not stop to let her cross but I was anxious to get to Kohls which was around the corner just out of sight.

Again, with this dream I felt I knew what it meant as soon as I woke up. The plaza represented my soul development. The crowd in the beginning were people or ides that got in my way and tried to deter my spiritual growth. But I have gotten in such a hurry to learn and grow and find meaning in my life that I'm possibly missing what I should be doing. That something has to do with healing which is represented by the lady with the walker.

SH, female

Response

Great use of the Universal Language of Mind to understand your dream! Congratulations! Here are a couple ideas to integrate into your observations and give more depth to your insights: first, the teenagers are immature aspects that relate to the goal you are striving to achieve however you see these parts of self as slowing you down. Maybe this is inexperience.

Secondly, you might be missing what you should be doing, yet consider this viewpoint. The lady with the walker could represent your own wisdom gained from experience that is hampered by your lack of attention and cultivation. Pay more attention to your own wisdom and you may find you have much more experience than you at first gave yourself credit for.

Keep up the good work, and begin helping others with their dreams too! It will help make the world a better place.

Wedding Day gone Awry

I have two dreams I would like to share.

One is sort of recurring, although in various forms. It has to do with my wedding day going awry. (I am not now, nor have I ever been married.)

In the most recent dream, *a guy I had dated (in real life) and am still friendly with, asked me to marry him. I accept and he tells me he wants to get married that day. I scramble around, trying to find a dress, make arrange-ments, etc. My mother panics and pulls out hot dogs and bratwurst from the freezer to feed the guests. It's all very stressful.*
    Meanwhile, my "fiance" is acting very non-chalant and quite cold toward me. At the last minute, when all the guests had arrived and I am nervously awaiting the ceremony, I tell him I do not want to marry him because I don't think he really loves me, and the wedding is off. Then I woke up....

SC, female

Response

This dream is reflecting your idea of commitment. Whatever in your life precipitated this subconscious feedback – your attitude about your performance at your job or making and keeping promises with friends – these dreams are about commitment. This dream indicates you consciously wait for a feeling or inner sense to move you and when the feeling leaves, you abandon the commitment. A good book to read would be **Motivation** by Dr. Pam Blosser.

Questions about Dreams

How long is the average dream? Any other sites I can visit to help answer questions?
JC, Female

Response

Studies show us we dream in cycles throughout a sleeping period. We go into deep levels of sleep very quickly initially, where the most rejuvenation can be experienced both in assimilation for the mind and reenergizing for the bodies. This brings the stage of sleep commonly known as REM, an acronym for rapid eye movement which describes the outwardly visible sign that someone is dreaming. REM usually lasts 1 to 4 minutes leading researchers to believe this is the length of the dreaming experience.

School of Metaphysics research revolves around the integration of the whole self and has been focussed on the content, meaning, and revelations possible in the dream state. Our research into levels of consciousness shows that time is measured differently in each level. Physical time is measured in a linear sense, by the rising and setting of the sun. Conscious time is measured by the experiences we have during the physical waking time. Subconscious time is by the understandings gained. More information on this is found in the book **Mechanics of Dreams** which is now out of print and available on this site.

Since the School of Metaphysics began researching dreams in the late '60's and since the advent of SOM's National Dream Hotline which began in 1989, many major universities have begun exploring this field more diligently and with greater seriousness. A search on university dream research will lead you to the current findings.

.

Tree Blown on Ground

Hi, my husband had a dream.

It started with him looking out a window at a pine tree that was blowing in the wind. There was a storm and the pine tree was swaying back and forth. It did that a couple of times then the pine tree was mashed to the ground after a hard gust of wind hit it. It broke in half when it hit the ground.

Could you tell him what this dream meant? Thanks. MJ, female (dream is her husband's)

Response

The Dreamer's Dictionary says trees represent subconscious existence. This dream is talking about your husband's state of being in his inner, subconscious mind. This is not necessarily what he shows and there is the tendency for him to remain separate from what is occurring inwardly. The day of the dream, he was being affected by rampant thoughts which were causing inner turmoil. Maybe he was worried about something at work or maybe you said something to him that his imagination got carried away with. Whatever it was, the dream is telling him how he is or is not effectively responding to his own life experience.

A good question for him to ask is "How are my conscious thoughts related to what I experience on a deeper level?" This will give his mind something positive to work on. **The Dreamer's Dictionary** suggests meditation as a means to still the outer mind thus becoming aware of the inner activity of thoughts and guidance.

96

Saving Snakes!

My father and I were fishing at a lake or some kind of body of water, the water started to get choppy or ripply looking, like a storm came up. But the water turned into a lake of snakes, and my father got a pitchfork and started to kill them, and I yelled at him not to kill the snakes.

Another dream: *A few friends of mine were going to my son's football game and we decided to walk, which would be a far walk. The ground was wet and there were puddles everywhere, as if it just rained. We were walking across the street from a lake, (this is a real lake and street by my home) and there were snakes everywhere; big snakes, little snakes, exotic looking snakes, colorful snakes. We had to watch where we walked because we didn't want to step on them. Well, one big snake started to cross the road, I said to my friends to help get the snake out of the road before it got hit by a car. They refused, so I pulled the snake by its tail off the road. My friends didn't want to walk anymore, so we went home and got the car and drove. I woke up!*

Is there a reason I dream of saving snakes???
TG, Female

Response

You are valuing wisdom in your life. These are dreams about creativity. You know what you value which is a great asset for you. Now you need to learn how to wield your whole Self to bring into life what you value and make yourself a reflection of that value. You sometimes feel alone in these thoughts, like other parts of your Self are working against you or not helping. Do not let self-imposed limitations keep you from creating the kind of life you desire. Set your goals high and move toward them each day, harnessing your intelligence and will power to live a fulfilling life made in your image.

WAKING UP in a Dream

I was sitting in a doctor's room when one of my husband's friends walked into the room with an exacto knife and sliced me open in the stomach area, took something out of me, placed it in tupperware, sealed it, and left. My friend, who I used to work with, came tearing into the room.

The next part of my dream skips to a hospital room.....I wake up in my dream. My friend is sitting there. All she says is that she was glad that she could help me out.

I woke up!!
IM, female

Response

This dream concerns the mental assimilation of experiences, digesting what has happened in your thoughts and actions. The stomach is the area of the solar plexus, where sympathetic and parasympathetic nervous systems operate. This area is where the fifth chakra, the Solar Plexus chakra, is active. Here are the mental energies of balance and the perpetual motion of life. For these reason the solar plexus is known as the seat of the conscious and subconscious mind, the union point for the soul. This dream indicates you are consciously assimilating in order to heal yourself, to bring together what up til now has been separate. Conscious assimilation is the doorway to wisdom. This dream encourages you to use yours.

Violence in Houses

There's a recurring theme I have in many of my dreams, it's houses. Houses I've never been to or seen, and all the houses usually have violence associated with them.

I dream that I'm looking at a house to buy or rent, and as I go room to room, I feel uncomfortable and then I'll walk into a room and find dead people. In one dream the bodies were floating in the pool in the backyard. Another one, I found bodies in a wicker laundry hamper, these bodies were chopped up.

In one dream, I opened a closet and there was blood covering the walls of the closet, no bodies though. One time I didn't even go in the house the terror I felt was so intense, I couldn't go inside. I can sense or feel that something violent has occurred in the house, and I usually wake up afraid.

There's one particular house that's been in numerous dreams. In the first dream of this house I found bodies in one of the bedrooms, under the bed. When I dream of this house now I'm living in there. This is the house I'm living in (and it's nothing like my home). This house has many bedrooms, in fact there's so many I haven't even been to all of them. When I dream of this house, I often discover new bedrooms. There's no more violence associated with this house, but when I pass the room where I found the dead people, I get apprehensive. Otherwise, I think I like the house.

TG, female

Response

You are trying to come to terms with your past. The houses are your mind and the dead people are aspects of self that changed a long time ago but you have held onto them. It's like going from elementary school to high school but something that happened in third grade still haunts you. Your body matured to 16 years but your hurt feelings stayed at the level of you at nine years. This at least gives you an idea to begin working with.

The dreams seem to progress. You are searching for truth in your past, then you search for truth in the present. This is significant because none of us can change what happened in the past, we can only change ourselves now in relation to the memory. The dream about the bedrooms indicates you are trying to come to terms with the past, you think you have but you are unsure. You need to assimilate what you think of the past experiences so these thoughts have a place in the present.

For instance your boss today may remind you of your second grade teacher, thus bringing up all kinds of emotions that belong in the past not in the present. In second grade you were afraid of your teacher, wanting to please. When you did please things were fine, when you didn't you were devastated. Now you want to please again, and the same old unresolved feelings are coming up again. You like your job and want to keep it so you are now motivated to figure this out.

In the final evolvement of these dreams you explore new parts of your mind (*new bedrooms*) finding your tendency to live in the past (*dead people*).

REOCCURRING *Baby who dies*

This dream has reoccurred 3 times in the last 6 months. It is a dream where

I have a baby in the hospital. I then leave the hospital, but leave the baby there for the weekend. One time I left the baby at home for the weekend. Every time I return from my weekend, thinking that someone, a nurse or family member would take care of the baby, upon my return, the baby is dead. The baby dies of malnutrition.

I am a 23 year old woman and I have no children and this dream seems kind of weird to me. The first time, I didn't think anything of it, but I have had this dream 3 times now and it is starting to worry me. Please help!

TJ, female

Response

Your dream is a good example of the evidence that dreams are indeed more than just a rehashing of the previous day's events.

Six months ago you had a new idea and a new way of life. Maybe you got married, moved to a new city, or started a career – whatever it was your lack of attention has changed it. For this dream to stop, you will need to go beyond this point in awareness. Either give up the idea, choosing to go back or to do something different or begin nurturing that idea so it can grow.

SHOT GUN *pointed at head*

The other night, I had a dream where I woke up and there was a man in my room pointing a rather large automatic shotgun at my head.

Now, I don't normally have these kinds of dreams and I was rather sick at the time. I am a 19 year old male who just started a new job....does this mean anything?

CJ, male

Response

This dream is talking about your attitudes, probably about your new job. You are learning at the job but it feels a bit overwhelming like you're being forced to make changes. Realize newness always brings change. Keep your goal in mind, being true to yourself. As long as the changes are productive, meet the challenge they propose. In this way you can take control of the change rather than remaining in a state of mind where you feel forced. This will increase your enjoyment of your work while enabling you to learn more quickly, thus becoming an asset to your employer.

The *Faceless Gunman*

I had a dream that

I was with my friend and this other person who I didn't see their face but I saw they were going to shoot her. Doing the one thing I could think of I jumped in the way and got shot. Later, after I recovered some what and went to school where nobody knew me, then this guy comes up to me and starts to talk about this girl who got shot to save her friend but he couldn't remember her name. He kept talking to me about myself and wouldn't let me tell him who I was. He had a face once but now he doesn't.

I dream of him often he always talks to me about me, each time about something else that I did earlier in the dream but I can never tell him about myself.

A.S., female

Response

Dreams reflect our state of conscious awareness usually the day of the dream. This dream reveals that you are in the midst of change in your life. The change is coming, threatening, but has yet to occur. You do not want the change to happen and are working diligently to avoid it. Whether this is good or bad you will have to decide based upon what you believe the change to be. Your dream indicates that you are not aware of the origin of the change (the faceless trigger man) or of how change comes about (the guy who doesn't tell you who he is).

Your subconscious mind is attempting to fulfill your desires but you have difficulty imaging them. It would be helpful for you to begin intentionally verbalizing your wants, telling others what you desire. This can be as simple as letting a friend know where you would like to eat or what movie you'd like to see. Based upon the imagery of your dream this could be very helpful for you will be establishing a greater rapport with yourself and others which will help your sense of control in your life.

The *Skeleton* in the *Garden*

I was in the back yard of what was my home in the dream. A group of us were near a garden in which I was digging, when I uncovered a skeleton. I was quite upset, it turned out one of the people in the group was detective. He soon disclosed that there were bodies hidden all over the house. I was pretty uneasy and wanted to get out of the house but he was telling me I should be safe sleeping in the living room.

What do you think ?
Receptionist, female

Response

You want to know how things work. The idea of this is a bit frightening to you, but your keen ability to reason and discern cause is a plus that keeps you curious and seeking. The day of this dream you were trying to figure out how something came about and eventually assimilated the experience. It may seem like strange imagery to tell you that it's time to explore consciousness and find out how your mind works, but that is what this dream is telling you. You might want to read Dr. Daniel Condron's book, **Superconscious Meditation**. It will tell you what those skeletons in the house are symbolizing!

Sitting & Waiting in VIETNAM

I have had this recurrent dream since I was a child.

I am sitting in still water with a gun in my hand..
watching always watching ... in an open area where
there is something to guard or watch. (Sort of like
being a soldier in waiting in Vietnam) It is warm it
makes me comfortable and it puts me to sleep.
Nothing ever happens I just sit and wait... that's all
I do.

What does this dream mean?
male; 35 yr.

Response

At the times you have this dream your inner self is
letting you know you are ready to make a change. The
still water is the receptive conscious mind, open and
waiting for a stimulus. The gun is a tool for change.
Before you can effectively use this receptive frame of
mind, you become distracted. It's like working diligently to attain a promotion, feeling certain you are
going to receive it, knowing you deserve it, and then
you miss an important meeting, so the promotion (the
change) never comes.   When the dream occurs look
for ways to make the change happen instead of waiting
for something else to cause it. The dream probably
comes when you could be accomplishing wonderful
things and making great discoveries.

French Toast

I wonder if you could tell me what this dream is about. I had it a couple of nights ago;

There is a big cart piled high with all different kinds of bread. The baker is telling me all the different kinds of bread he has baked. He gives me a slice of a particular kind. I don't eat it. He then shows me a really interestingly shaped bread and I ask him what it is used for. He says, French toast. Then he encourages me to try the piece I have in my hand. I do and it tastes sweet! I actually taste the sweetness of the bread. He had not told me that it was going to be sweet.

I dream in vivid Technicolor, but never have tasted anything! Is this unusual?

Thank you, M*

Response

You are relishing what you are learning. That's the message in your dream. As long as it is pleasant and appealing, you enjoy learning otherwise you give little attention to the wide berth of learning opportunities present.

Dreaming in color indicates the level of subconscious mind you are dreaming in. Technicolor dreams are in the Lower Astral Level of Consciousness. This is the part of mind where your ideas begin to become physically recognizable, taking on the distinct characteristics that eventually make people, places, and things seemingly different. For instance, male and female split, light separates into the colors of the rainbow. For more information on the divisions of mind and levels of consciousness study Dr. Daniel Condron's book based on three decades of research and teaching, **Superconscious Meditation**.

Your keen attention to taste in this dream indicates a greater degree of awareness in your dream state. In other words, you are beginning lucid dreaming. This is a skill that can be taught and learned, and I would encourage you to investigate the Mastery of Consciousness course taught at the School of Metaphysics.

Cannibalistic *GHOSTS*

I am in Church grounds (the church I am attending currently) surrounded by many, many ghosts...ghosts in women form are all around me. I'm terribly scared. I am a ghost too. I'm scared especially of these 2 women ghosts who seem cannibalistic. In fact one of them (who is my aunt) is eating human flesh. I'm terrified. Its night time, I was supposed to go to the new movie "Unbreakable" and I hear that this movie is all about ghosts.

The Dreamer's Dictionary says ghosts are "inner level bodies"--I don't understand this term relating to my dream---it sounds vague. I understand we have bodies in the inner realms. But what exactly is the dream telling me? Please clarify.

I'm so tired of dreaming of ghosts. I have dreamt of ghosts all my life over and over. I'm so tired of being scared of ghosts in my dreams. Please help. Thanks so much for reading my request.

N, female

Response

Your ghosts are the unfulfilled desires that you have abandoned throughout your life, ideas you allowed to fall by the wayside for one reason or another that hold meaning for you, particularly spiritually. If you want to be free of this haunting you will need to either release the desires from your mind or take action to fulfill them. One of these unfulfilled desires is something you have in common with your aunt. Determine what aspect of yourself she represents and you will have an idea of what this desire is.

Night to Day Dream about a
CAR WRECK

For the last 2 months every night I have a dream about my girlfriend, whom is married, having a car wreck and being in the hospital. Every time the dream is the same. Now I daydream the same thing and when I'm around her I feel terrible sad thinking that the present may be the last time I ever see her. I'll give you my dream just as it happens. Please help me find some answers as this is bothering me something terrible.

I start dreaming by seeing her husband's SUV upside on the side of the road with lots of red flashing lights around it. Although not one time have I seen an ambulance or evidence that anyone is in the SUV.

The next step to my dream I appear at a hospital that looks really familiar to me. As I get off the elevator I see her husband standing in the waiting room laughing and joking around with people. I go to him, and as I go i notice a familiar looking blue chair behind him, I ask him where she is and he tells me to get lost I can't see her. I grab him by the shirt push him down in the chair and tell him to shut up that i'm going to find her and find out just what is going on.

I proceed through to stainless steel doors that seem to lead to Intensive Care rooms. I look in every room until i find the one that she is in. I go in and she's all bandaged up and is on a respirator. A nurse, the same nurse every time, comes in and! ask me if I'm family I say no and she says you're going to have to leave I tell her i'm not leaving and she says she is going to call security. I tell her to do what she needs to do. End of dream.

I wake up every time sweating and scared. Sometimes I go back to sleep and dream the same thing over and over again. Now I think about it all day. As a matter of fact its getting worse, its like i'm getting use to the fact that something is going to happen.

Please tell me what this is all about, its driving me crazy and I'm scared for my lover.
Thank You
C*

Response

This is a health dream, not about your married lover but about YOU and your health. Your state of mind has affected your physical health as evidenced by the wrecked SUV. The attempts to heal are similar to those you have taken before, you try to force your inner self to fulfill your desires. Central to this health crises is the aspect symbolized by the girl. She is a part of you that weakens your will power, thereby causing you to rely upon external motivation for discipline.

This is an intricate dream with potentially much depth for you if you can separate your conscious fears from the dream message itself. A place to begin is to take an inventory of your state of health. Beyond the commonplace obvious...diet....no smoking....explore these areas.... Integrative practices such as yoga or rebirthing (both under the tutelage of experienced teachers) can bring great healing of mind and body. You need a way to consciously direct your life force, either of these can supply it. A good book to read is **First Opinion: Wholistic Health Care in the 21st Century.**

Electrical Malfunction....

My name is H* and I have many unusual dreams especially about Russia. One dream actually occurred in real life 5 months after I dreamed it, but it was unimportant. I have had one dream in the front of my mind for the past year and I ask people to give me their opinion but they never give me any type of response. Anyway, here it is:

There is a bolt of electricity. Then I watch as three Russian officers walk a short distance down a runway to a convoy of military trucks parked at the end. The land around them is green but very barren and it must be winter because they are wearing gray coats. Then I know that they are testing some kind of weapons system and there was an electrical malfunction.

I have no idea what this means and I have thought about it for a year. I can still visualize my way through it. PLEASE give me some sort of response. Thank you.

Response

It is relative to the meaning of this dream whether you do or have ever lived in Russia. If Russia is a foreign country to you its presence in your dreams indicates times you are at a loss to understand yourself or your experiences. Foreign countries in dreams symbolize unfamiliar conditions of mind. This occurs often in our changing lives -- a new baby in your life brings many new and unfamiliar frames of mind or an unfavorable health diagnosis can produce this. Whether something you want to keep or want to change in the way you are thinking, when foreign countries show up in your dream it indicates unfamiliar or alien conditions of mind.

The dream you relate indicates you have recently experienced energy in your life that you do not know how to interpret because it is new to you. This could be consciously induced through yoga or martial arts, or unconsciously induced through medical drugs. It could be from changes in your life, such as a move to a new city or falling in love or experiencing a death of a loved one. How it fits into your life, you will need to determine. What is most important is determining what the Russian element is and what it signifies when it appears in your dreams. If Russia is not your homeland, then every time it appears in your dream ask yourself "What have I experienced lately that has challenged by sense of security and stability?" When you can identify what that is, you will be on your way to understanding the message your subconscious mind seeks to get across.

Six Months Pregnant...
but only in the dream

Hi! I just wanted to share a dream that I keep having with you. Maybe you can see if anyone else is having this dream. It's kind of strange, but here goes:

I am getting out of a car full of family and friends and I'm going into a house. The first time I dreamed it, I was going into the basement of a house, unfinished house with no ceiling or roof. And, I was pregnant...about 6 months or so. The second time I had the dream we had moved up to the ground floor of the unfinished house with no ceiling and I was still about 6 months pregnant. There were friends and family all around. My dad asked me to come upstairs but I told him I couldn't because I was pregnant and there was nothing to hold on to on the stairs. The next time I dreamed about this, all my family, friends and myself (still pregnant) were leaving this house and going next door. My friends were all carrying mattresses...there were about 4-5 mattresses in this unfinished house. We were going to the house next door, which did have a ceiling but was very plain and unfinished as well.

Just a little background...I have never been pregnant, I'm not even married. I do want to have a child, but now is not a good time. I have also, never bought or had a house built. I also live 6 hours from my parents, family and friends. I'm unsure of the meaning of this dream! Why do I dream I'm pregnant? What does a house without a ceiling/roof mean? Why did I start in the basement then only move to the ground floor the next time? Will I go upstairs next time? What does this dream mean?
Just thought you may want to add this to your research!
Thanks
L., female

Response

Pregnancy dreams indicate a new idea that you are creating. It is gestating in your mind, not in your physical life yet. Your first dream indicates a willingness to explore what has been unconscious, things you have been unaware of (basement). The next dream indicates progress as you are exploring your conscious, waking mind – the way you see the world, what you want in it and from it, etc. The fact that your houses are unfinished means you see yourself as a work in progress, your mind as something to be created and discovered. When your dad which symbolizes your superconscious mind wants you to go upstairs your dream is saying you are stimulated to explore deeper parts of self but hold back because of this impending new idea.

Visiting the next door house indicates you are continuing to explore the possibilities of your mind, noting tools for assimilation (the mattresses). An example of such a tool would be your memory or sleep or contemplation.

Your dreams indicate you are embarking upon a new phase of your life where you are willing to make self discoveries. Cultivate this awareness for it can serve you well all the days of your life. May you always see the world with fresh eyes and fill that dream-house with whatever furniture you find desirable!

ANGRY CATS

I recently dreamed that

I was in my mother's house (she is 85) when a bunch of angry cats came in and were running around in an apparent heat run. However, in the middle of the scurry they were tearing at a small lap dog.

Two years ago in April my father died and in December the same year my mother's cat died trying to give birth. The cat was full grown but small in stature. My mother is lonely now and I am being advised to get her a cat as a companion.

CM, female

Response

This dream is about you, the dreamer. Your subconscious mind is giving you a message about the state of your awareness. This message concerns how habitual ways of thinking (cats and dog) about your own inner authority are disrupting your sense of spirituality. You'll need to decide just what the dream is referring to....it could be you are being stimulated by events in your life to review your religious/spiritual beliefs or it could be you are realizing your spiritual ideals are not your own but something you accepted long ago. Something like that. It might help to bring your ideas into the present day, to give more thought to how your spirituality serves you and others.

114

Dreams that Foretell the Future

Hello
I saw an article about the School of Metaphysics and the dream hotline. What do you know about people who have reoccurring dreams which then come true? What percentage of the population has experienced this? Someone once told me it means you are using a larger percentage of your brain than others. The dreams do appear to happen most often during times when I am using my brain a lot at work doing creative research. If you would like to hear about some of the episodes, I can tell you about some of them.

Thanks
GPM, male

Response

We've seen some polling data concerning subconscious activity – like dreaming in general or esp and the like – but nothing specifically in the precognitive dream arena. Hopefully we can use this website to change this in the next few years. From thirty years of teaching metaphysics to literally 1000's of people, the percentage of precognitive dreams falls near 60%. You must keep in mind two factors: 1] the fineness of attention to dream experiences put forth by those attracted to the School of Metaphysics and its study, and 2] the natural enhanced development of subconscious skills resulting from mental disciplines and spiritual practices. Both of these factors increase both the probability of precognitive dreams and the rate of recall. Without doubt more of the mind is being used and therefore more of the physical brain capacity is being called upon as well. Brainwave research is just one of the areas we hope to develop here on the campus of the College of Metaphysics.

We are most interested in dreams of this (and other) nature. Please feel free to send them to us or to contact us at world headquarters: 1-417-345-8411.

THE DARK...

What does it mean to have dreams where it's dark?
When I was younger about 10 or so I use to have
nightmares where it was all dark in my house. I
would always go and try to find the light switch but
when I went to flick the switch the lights wouldn't
go on. There was also someone else in my house
with me. I would always try to escape from them .
In my dream they always appeared as a dark
shadow but I never ever saw their face. Does this
mean that I was afraid of someone?

JH, Female

Response

The Dreamer's Dictionary identifies darkness as
ignorance. Ignorance does not imply mental insuffi-
ciency or stupidity. It implies an active state of ignoring what is present or available to the dreamer. Fear
of the dark is a common anxiety for children. They
want to know everything, and so reach for experience.
In order for us to use the sense most relied upon – sight
– there must be light. The desire to consciously see our
physical world is an outer manifestation of our desire
for the inner light of awareness. This was present in
you at age 10. You were seeking to use your mind for
greater awareness and having trouble making the
connections. Because you couldn't identify (dark
faces) what was happening in your consciousness you
didn't know what to do (fear of the unknown).

This time of life shapes much of what we will do
the rest of our lives. From 10 to 14 is the time we
become aware of individual responsibility to self and
others and the power of our thoughts to create our
reality. Physically it is manifested as puberty, mentally it is the arousal of Kundalini. The more we can
help our children understand the inner transition occurring during these years, the better creators they will
become.

For you, now as an adult, you remember these
dreams because light – awareness – is still important
to you. The eternal now is the time learn and grow.
You might want to join us each day in saying the
Prayer for Enlightenment around the World. It is a
wonderful way to cause your light to fill you and
expand throughout the Earth.

A DOOZIE…Sister's Weird Dream

My sister, Jody just sent me this horrendous dream...what a doozie! It's not funny by any means, but I almost peed myself reading it. This could be a textbook example of something!

I dreamed of being diagnosed with an incurable disease, not sure which one, didn't matter. The kids and Pete were in the know about my condition, and I was not suffering physically at the time. The kids and Pete decided to have a practical discussion with me about my situation, and it was decided quite democratically that since I was going to die anyways, they were going to help me plan my burial. They were quite matter-of-fact about everything, and decided that I should begin being buried while I could still walk. That would save them from having to wait on me during the late stages of my illness and then by the time I died, I'd be completely buried. So, it was in the best interests of the majority of the household that I should agree to having myself buried alive.

They set about planning their new space -- newly purchased add-on rooms to the house in Libertyville -- purchase with the money from my insurance policy. Their dad would get a loan to start the project ... to be paid off at the event of my incumbent death. They asked me to step into a hole in the wall -- my height, about the size of a coffin.

They began bricking me into the wall ... one brick at a time. They were serious about their work, and while not laughing and cracking jokes, they were preoccupied with everyday matters and paid me little attention .. more a nuisance at not being able to go out and play than any-thing else.

Then I awoke and vomited.

JH, female

Response

The fact that the content of dreams can actually make you physically ill, which this dream apparently did to your sister, is a testament to the reality of our thoughts. I hope this interpretation eases her mind.

Not long ago one of our teachers had a similar dream in that she was being buried alive. The situation was a bit different, she was actually in the grave and people were throwing dirt on her, but that's her story. I share it to let you know you are not the only person who has dreamed such a dream.

Death in a dream indicates change. The entire theme of your dream is an impending change that is happening to you. What this is you will have to determine by examining what occurred in your life the day of your dream or the day before. Dreams are always timely feedback messages. What is most important is the incurable disease. Disease in a dream indicates unproductive attitudes held by the dreamer. This is mental and/or emotional distress, discomfort, and distemper that is causing you to change. This could be good or bad depending upon how it fits into your life. (For example: A medical scare that causes you to take better care of yourself could be considered good; an emotional depression that steals the joy from your life could be seen as bad).

The aspects closest to you (the kids and Pete) are helping you make this change as symbolized by helping to bury you. Since you haven't made the change yet, you find this alarming or repulsive. These aspects of you see great value (insurance money) in the impending change that will enable your mind to expand (add-ons). They are continuing to move in the direction of the change which you are reluctant to make.

Determine which change the dream is telling you about, go ahead and make it, and you will be able to move forward in your life without fear and without regret.

It was probably one of the worst dream experiences you've ever had but its message is potent.

119

A dream that lingers...

Last week i had a dream that affected me greatly, even now almost seven days later, i can recall it distinctly.

It began in a place that was like being in the mountains, in front of me was a very clear creek, not really big enough to be counted as a river, and didn't have obnoxiously flowing water. On the other side of the creek was a group of horses, they would have to have been wild, mainly all of which were mostly solid colors but each horse differed from white to dark. They basically stood at the bottom of a mountain peak, but we were not at the bottom of the mountains. To the left you could see more peaks in the distance, at which there was an awesome sunset taking place putting the rest of my surroundings in that mysterious twilight glow. Behind stood a large house. Not big enough to be obscenely huge, but not some poor mans shack by any means.

Getting back to the horses, there was a white one that was basically in charge of the group, while the others sipping from the creek this one looked me directly in the eye and we held that for a few minutes. Obviously some type of communication had taken place, but what exactly I don't know for sure. Nothing confrontational in any way, and i am going to have to go as far as saying spiritual in nature. Then as if our "conversation" was over i turned around and went back into the house.

Inside there was a party going on, nobody i recognized, but within the dream we were all pals and friends. Something like a bunch of college pals getting together like they inevitably do. The party was no big deal because the dining room was on the backside of the house where it had huge windows and I could sit down and watch the horses across the way. Then a girl came in, again not recognizing her as someone i know in my waking reality, i knew her within in the dream as being my significant other. We embraced each other passionately, but not in a sexual way, and watched the horses together. She didn't seem to know what had happened between me and the group's leader, but just held me tight and brought a very warm and comfortable natural smile to me. Right then the alarm clock went off and i had to begin my day.

Any how i thought i would submit this, because again it had affected me greatly, and not negatively as of yet, where nothing of this sort has happened in a very long time. I do have a few ideas as of the meaning and circumstances there within. Any help though is greatly appreciated, a second opinion is truly a great tool. Thank you for taking your time to read through this, and to any advice or thoughts that you have.

Sincerely

MH, Male, Wyoming

Response

This dream is feedback concerning a challenge (mountains) in your life (creek). You have things to learn and your will (horses) is essential to learning the lessons. You have been looking at past opportunities (left, sunset) with new awarenesses and this has led to realizations about you (large house). Will power is predominant and you are aware of this. You have a strong sense of the role determination has played in your life.

Now you are becoming aware of unknown aspects of yourself that see life from a perspective differing from the one you hold (people at the party). Even midst these aspects you hold your attention on your will and as a result you are becoming aware of a subconscious aspect that is compatible to you, one that will help you fulfill your desires.

Concentration was a big theme in meeting this day's challenge. Remember what happened the day of the dream and the interpretation will be more useful to you. Hope this sheds additional light.

The PEOPLE in my car

Hello,

My name is P*...I am new to this site...however i am very fascinated with it...I have recently separated from my husband...after an eleven yr. marriage...I have began dreaming again...it has been so long since i really dreamed...or could remember my dreams...I used to look forward to my dreams...it was away that told me what is going to happen...but it has been so long that my powers have diminished in understanding what my dreams are telling me now...

I had a dream last night...in where I was walking to my car...that was parked parallel... I never park parallel...I was leaving the college that I am now attending as a student...in my dream I was carrying my books...and it was at night time...i never carry my books i have a book bag...and i attend the university during the day...well anyway...in my dream i noticed that they are people trying to get into my car...i go right up to my car...the passenger door was open...and i said we had better hurry before the bitch comes back for her car...now i am not an assertive person...passive aggressive is my personality trait...when i had said this...they were 2 guys and 1 girl...and 1 guy in the driver seat...after i had spoken the guys left without argument...but the female...had to be persuaded but with verbal force...also, in my dream there was a person looking onward...he was male also...he did not intervene in anyway...he just observed...

Now at first this dream was disturbing to me...but i am trying to understand what my subconscious is trying to tell me...Can you help with the interpretation of this dream...I maybe wrong, but i think that my body is getting ready to have some sort of change...i am hoping positive change...but there are going to be obstacles in my way...anticipating your thoughts and interpretations...
Thanks so much for reading...P, female

122

Response

Dream droughts – that's what a student of mine used to call them – are times in our lives when we don't recall dream experiences. The experiences are happening, we just don't consciously remember them. Remembering your dreams following your separation from your husband may be a cause and effect relationship, you will need to decide. Sometimes it is easier for people who sleep alone to remember dreams. They are not distracted by another or concerned about waking them when they turn on the light to record their dreams. Things of this nature. Just the newness can bring a heightened sense of awareness that makes recalling dreams easier. At any rate we're glad you are remembering your dreams again and hope you will continue the rest of your days.

The message in the dream you send to us revolves around how you think about and treat your own body. The car in your dream is your physical body. You are gaining knowledge, learning about how your mind and body work together, but when it comes to applying what you are learning you are finding this difficult. There are unknown conscious and subconscious aspects that are actively interfering with your capacity to use what you are learning for your own benefit. You are unaware of these aspects but they are self-degrading, working against you and that is why your subconscious mind is bringing them to your attention in this dream.

Suggestions...make a conscious effort to give more loving, healthful attention to your body. How you treat your body tends toward the unconscious so you probably tend to run it into the ground or at least take it for granted. Start appreciating your body more, even pamper it for a while and see what happens. As a chiropractic pamphlet once noted: "if you wear out your body, where are you going to live?" Yes, you'll still continue on as a soul, but while you're here on earth it's ever so helpful to have fully functional equipment for your mind to use!

123

SWIMMING NUNS

See if you can help me with this one.

Each day a nun comes to my house to use the swimming pool in my backyard. Each nun first takes a kiwi fruit out of my refrigerator before she goes outside. I don't really see their faces, just the generic nun with the usual traditional dress. The thing is, every day as a nun comes to eat the kiwi fruit and use the swimming pool she dies. No specifics on how she dies and I don't see her dead, just the same thing each day. My fiancée finally suggests after several days of this that I should have the kiwi fruits tested at a toxicology clinic. So I cut one open and I remember how juicy and colorful it was, and I cut a small piece out of it, and the piece falls to the floor. When I look down, my fiancée's basset hound is gobbling it up. I remember feeling panicked and helpless and I woke up very suddenly then.

Some background: I'm a 42 year old male who is about to get re-married. She's Catholic and I'm Protestant but that difference is not really an important issue in our relationship. I don't really see nuns at all in my life so I'm not sure the significance there. I don't even have a swimming pool and I can't imagine seeing a nun in one. There was no sinister feeling at all in the dream and no sexual feelings of any kind. I did have an empathetic feeling each time I would hear that a nun had died and the dreadful feeling when the dog ate the piece on the floor. Any help would be much appreciated.
J* from OK.

Response

We must say this is a unique dream. It is a message about how you view your own divinity as symbolized by the nuns (who represent superconscious aspects of you). Your subconscious mind is telling you your inner authority from knowledge gained (kiwi, a food) is coming out into your everyday life (swimming pool) and changing (nun dies) the way you understand that inner authority. Whatever concepts you have held about your own spirituality are changing again and again. This can be most productive because change always brings about new opportunities for growth and fulfillment.

Your subconscious mind (in the form of your fiancee) encourages you to look for the cause of these changes. You look for cause in the knowledge you have gleaned. In other words, you have a habit (basset hound) of giving credit, and probably blame, to outer authority rather than embracing the understanding control personal experience brings.

A good response on your part to this dream message would be to consciously choose to expand your thoughts about spirituality and divinity. You say it's not an issue in your impending marriage and certainly does not have to become one in a detrimental sense. What metaphysical thoughts give us is understanding of ourselves and our world beyond the material, physical plane. Your dream says this is important to you now. As a suggestion, you might want to find ways to live/practice your spiritual ideals – be it daily meditation, prayer, walks in the wood or by the water. This will enable you to determine the direction of the changes you are experiencing.

Snakes & Rats

I had a dream that i was in my bedroom, in my mother's house (where i was living when i had this dream). On one side of my bedroom i had a snake cage with a couple snakes in it, and on the other side i had a cage with some rats in it. The snakes and rats were my pets. Some of the rats were escaping out of the cage, so i went to catch them and put them back. Then I realized that some of the snakes had escaped too. I was rushing to catch all the animals and put them back, because I was afraid that some of the snakes would eat my rats. Suddenly, i saw that there were snakes and rats everywhere. The started to multiply rapidly, and before I knew it I was completely surrounded by rats & snakes I felt upset and overwhelmed, and thought to myself, "how am i going to put them all back in their cages?"

Then i got this eerie feeling of suspense. I turned and looked over my shoulder, and saw this bright white light shining through my window (which was open) from outside. An angel stepped through the window into my bedroom, and my room was filled with a bright light. I was extremely frightened. I fell down to my knees and covered my head so that i couldn't see it. The angel spoke to me. It said, "I do not have an answer for you." I looked up at it. It floated about a foot off the ground. I really could not see his face very well because it was surrounded by bright light. But I believed that it was the archangel Michael. Then there was quiet and suspense again, and the angel slowly drifted back out the window, and left. I felt someone's presence, so i turned around and looked at my bedroom door which was cracked open. My mother was peeking around behind it. She had seen the whole incident. I went up to her and said, "Did you see what happened?" and she said yes. Then we were both at a loss for words.

We went downstairs. The dream seemed to change direction at this point. The rest is a hazy story about my mother living as a prostitute. She would be having sex with her clients in her room. It was nighttime. After some men left her room, I went in there and found her lying naked in her bed, she was disoriented and her mouth was full of blue ink. The men had poisoned her by making her drink the ink. I wrapped her in sheets and called an ambulance. The paramedics came and got her and carried her away. I forgot the rest.

I am a 19-year-old girl from CA

Response

This dream is talking about your superconscious mind (mother's house, as well as later symbols of angel, mother). Your sense of wisdom is habitual, compulsive, and therefore beyond your control as symbolized by the snakes, rats, and escape from their cages. You are no longer at peace with how you used to understand wisdom, now there are new awarenesses entering your life (light and angel). The reason the angel does not have an answer for you is because you will need to form the new identity. Your current ideas of spirituality are no longer enough for you.

What needs to change is reflected in the final part of the dream concerning your mother as prostitute. Symbolically, what needs to change is the way you see superconscious mind, how you know your own divinity. The lack of commitment in this regard is causing you to defile your own sense of spirituality. You are becoming honest about this and are seeking help to cause your own healing.

Physically speaking, this dream could be quite troubling, but in the Universal Language of Mind it reveals a transition in the dreamer's spiritual reality. For ideas that will stimulate a new way of knowing yourself spirituality check out www.som.org our parent website. Look for the *Revelation of God in Man* and *Meditation*.

Protecting CHILDREN

I have this recurring dream every once in a while that
haunts me over and over again....

*I dream that I am viciously killing adults with ma-
chine guns. I am sweating (in my dream) and there is
fire all over. I am protecting children of all ages. I am
hiding them from these bad people. The colors that
stand out in my dreams are darkness/blackness and
fire. I will go to every extent it takes to protect these
children.*

I know the dream seems obvious but I am curious to what
you think. Thank you for taking the time to read this
dream.
CL, female

Response
You are causing change (killing), intentionally. Older
aspects (adults) of yourself are being changed and it is
causing you to see everything (fire) in a different way.
The motive for the change is probably the new ideas you
want to nurture symbolized by the children. Our physical
life is for learning and growing in awareness so our soul
can progress in enlightenment. When we use the physical world for this purpose we do cause change. We
continually embrace new learning which sometimes
means letting go of old ways of thinking and doing. You
value your new ways and are courageous enough to
change the old that are working against your growth.
Congratulations!

Recurring Childhood Dreams.....
PAST LIFE MEMORIES

When I was a child (I am now 59), I had the same dreams over and over of a huge spiral hanging over my head which would get closer and closer until I felt as if I were going to smother. I would always awake frightened.

A few years ago I started reading novels about the first inhabitants of our continent and found this same spiral used over and over in these stories. I became fascinated with learning about these peoples and their customs. In fact, last fall while visiting in New Mexico, we made a special trip to Chaco Canyon to see the ruins there. On some level I seem to be able to relate to these people, but how I don't know. Any thoughts about this? When I was a child, I knew nothing about Indians or their religious symbols.

I frequently--well nightly--dream about many, many things, people, and places that I've never seen. I usually dream about being in a town or several big buildings with lots of people doing strange things and quite often I dream about being in or around water, but I am prevented from getting around some natural or man-made obstruc-tion. Quite often I dream about the house I grew up in, but it never looks the same. I even dream when I take afternoon naps!! I do like being in clear, shallow water for snorkeling; I am a nature lover, and I do have a huge, fertile imagination.

And in the past few years, I have become very interested in religion. I am not presently going to church, but I do like to read books that answer "how could that have happened?" or "was that right?" I am presently read Alan Dershowitz's latest book **Genesis of Justice**, that I find fascinating. I would be interested in a response and in participating in any research in this area of dreams if possible. I read an article in today's newspaper about dreams. This is how I got your website.

FD, female

Response

The spiral you saw as a child before awakening, was your own spirit form moving out of the inner levels of consciousness returning back into your physical body lying in bed. For some people spirit appears as a huge bird or is symbolized as falling in a dream. Since you didn't know what it was and no one could tell you, you learned to be frightened of this natural mind-happening. Now, you might look for it again so you can eliminate the fear and replace it with adult-curiosity.

The spiral shows how the energy moves within the inner levels of mind. It is a common symbol around the world to show forward motion. Since subconscious mind is where the Akashic Records are found, it is entirely possible you were remembering an experience from another time and place. (For more on Akashic Records and Intuitive Past Life accounts go to www.som.org)

The strong familiarity sense you experienced while reading, and particularly visiting, also support this conclusion. A Past Life Profile might be further verification, especially in the significance of the symbol to you.

The snippets of other dreams indicate the many opportunities you have for learning (*towns*), often unfamiliar (*people*), in your everyday life (*water*). Dreaming of the house you grew up in that never looks the same symbolizes how you change your mind. You have a natural inclination toward your subconscious mind that it would be worth your time to investigate and cultivate.

Strange Bridges *to* Cross

I have been having dreams in which I am on a journey and in one part of the journey I have to cross over a bridge. The weather is always very cold and the sea or body of water very turbulent. I am always going someplace familiar, usually Colorado, which is strange because there is no sea close by. I run into people I know, like my sons, friends or my late husband.

The bridges I have to cross are strange. One was like the boom of a crane and I had to crawl across on my hands and knees. I had to go back and forth several times to bring people over. One bridge was made of thick conveyer belt type material that would buckle and sway when I tried to cross. The bridges are never passable by vehicle so I have to crawl across.

When I get to the other side, I have no transportation. The images are very clear and the towns have precise detail and I interact with people. I never seem to get to my destination. After the bridges either my new vehicle (car or truck) breaks down, I can't get a ride or the passes in the mountains are closed.

One night I finally got to Denver on a bus but then couldn't get a ride so I rode a big wheel through the snow with only a tee shirt on. I met a friend in the ladies room at a parking garage and asked her if my thighs were fat!

I will suddenly waken with a fast beating heart. What could this mean?
PS, female

Response

Bridges in a dream symbolize a way for the dreamer to move through his life. This indicates the goals the dreamer has set that enables her to easily and quickly accomplish objectives. If the bridge ends, this symbolizes the need for new goals to be created by the dreamer.

Your bridge dreams indicate your mental frame of mind is what is important in how you conduct your life. You have been willing to put out great effort at times in your life, but you always seem to fall short of accomplishing your objectives or having what you want in life. Sickness or some other obstacle seems to get in your way.

With the help of an organization (could be your church, a club, or informal group of friends) you finally have obtained a life goal in large part because you've become more open and honest about the power of your creative abilities. In that final dream, you were still concerned about your capacity to move forward in life.

Since bridge dreams are common to you, here are some thoughts that may help. Ask yourself, "Are the goals I have set for myself taking me where I want to go? Do they reflect the person I am and want to become?" Goals in life give the mind a direction and offer a place for the mind's energies to be used. Set your goals high, including the betterment of Self and others in your thinking. Make sure your present-day thoughts and actions are in alignment with your goals, thus bringing you closer to their fulfillment. From your dreams it seems that the more you can involve yourself with other people, the more likely you are to accomplish what you set out to. Interact! Teach! Give! Love! These are strengths in moving us through life.

My Baby Girl Falling

I had a horrible dream of my then 2 year old daughter falling to her death.

We were in a nuclear facility on a tour. We sat down in some desks for classroom discussion and the floor suddenly fell away between the desks. (The desks were now on pedestals) We were 50ft or so in the air. My little girl was sitting in a desk beside me when this happened and she tried to walk over to me, and fell to her death. I distinctly remember hearing her hit with a thud and moan in terrible agony.

What does this horrible nightmare mean?

Response

This dream is about how you use energy. The energy could be your own vitality or a nonpersonal form such as money. As always, you will need to determine how the interpretation fits into your life. What you have been learning about energy changed in the past day or so before this dream (maybe you took a new vitamin or got a "bad" medical diagnosis, maybe you won the lottery or lost your job). Whatever it is, the ideas you held that previously supported the way you see this energy no longer hold truth for you and as a result the new conscious idea (symbolized by your daughter who falls to her death) you favored has also changed.

To understand this, or any other dream, remember what was happening in your life the day of or before the dream. This is most likely what the dream message is pertaining to. Find out what energy your dream is talking about and it will be easier to see how and what has changed, including the idea symbolized by your baby girl.

The best part about this dream is the fact that it falls into one of those "could never happen" categories of dreams, so you know it is not precognitive. Do not be afraid for your child, love her and care for her, realizing your dream is your own.

134

Kidnapped!

I am very confused about a dream I keep having. I have this dream several times a month and have been having it for about 3 or so years.

I dream that I've been kidnapped and taken to a house. I can see this house very clearly and the house is about 8 miles away from my house, I pass it everyday approx. 4 times a day, although I've never been in this house. I can never see the face of the person who is keeping me there, and the only furniture in the house that I ever see is a coffee table and a fireplace. the walls are a dirty white, and there are blinds covering all the windows.

This is as far as the dream goes. I never remember anything else about it. Please help me, this really bothers me.

Thank You,

S*

Response

This dream says during your day you felt you were being forced to explore a part of mind that was unfamiliar to you. This part of you is foreign, ill-kept and isolated. This could be an old memory you've been repressing, not wanting to remember, or a reaction to a situation in your life now that you find intimidating or repulsive. Maybe you had to fire someone at work. Or maybe you were expected to know something you do not. Whatever it was, when you identify it you'll solve the mystery of this dream and begin taking back control of yourself. You won't be kidnapped anymore!

CAN'T SLOW DOWN, faster, faster.....

I have had a recurring dream during my life of being in a vehicle, usually a truck, my father's truck or a big truck, that is accelerating out of control, once even backwards. I try to stop or slow down by using the brakes or swerving side to side without results, and in many cases just go faster and faster. My heart is racing as well fearing impending death. I become even more anxious as my coordination to stop the vehicle leaves me feeling helpless actually paralyzed with fear not being able to prevent my fate from occurring.

I wake up in a sweat with my heart about to explode out from my chest. I hate this, i hate it. Please help. It has even caused me anxiety as I drive during waking hours. Thanks DF, male

Response

First of all, your dream is not about driving, or trucks, or your brakes. Dreams are a reflection of your conscious awareness, your conscious thoughts. The dream is about how you are moving down your path in life (road), and in this case you are "accelerating out of control" and are having trouble "putting on the brakes." The truck represents your physical body, so this careening down your path in life without slowing and resting adequately will wear upon your physical body if unchecked. Feeling helpless means you need to use your imagination in directing your life and how you move from experience to experience through choice--purposeful choice.

Fearing death means you are resisting impending change in your life. Look for the learning opportunities in what is occurring around you and what you're going through. That will turn your fear into curiosity, excitement or purposefulness, and eventually understanding of the lesson involved.

Take care of your health through all of this! If we can serve you in any other way, please let us know.

136

Tree of Athena

This was the first time I sent anything to you. A couple of nights ago I saw this wonderful dream:
I was in a blooming garden, sitting on a branch of a beautiful tree. In the dream I was 100% sure that this tree was called the 'tree of Athena.'
Nothing remarkable about the dream except for the fact that I have never heard that such a thing (tree of Athena) existed. I was so curious that I actually searched for it on the Internet. The results showed that the tree of Athena actually exists (in fact, it is an olive tree). The search results also included your school of metaphysics, so I thought it would be fun to send this to you and ask for an interpretation. What do you say?
J, female

Response

Anyone who would search the internet looking for confirmation of something in her dream possess an inquisitive mind and industrious spirit. You are to be congratulated! Since everything works according to Universal Law, and nothing is by chance or coincidence, we are happy that Law led you to us.

You may not have consciously known of the tree of Athena but your subconscious mind working outside the limits of your conscious physical mind does. Your subconscious mind chose this tree as a symbol in your dream so you would remember the message. It seems appropriate to also consider why Athena would be a symbol in your dream. Athena was a Greek goddess who sprung full grown from her father, Zeus's head. She is described as the goddess of wisdom.

Since dream gardens indicate the imaged thoughts the dreamer is impressing in subconscious existence this dream would be speaking to the wisdom available within your subconscious mind.

137

Robbing a Bank....

I have always had very vivid dreams which I can usually remember. Some have a very Sci Fi feeling, some are very choppy but most are just weird. I have had a recurring dream which I have found to be pretty common.

I am back in college and I forget where my classes are or I am teaching again and I can't find my class. The dream is spent looking for my classes. I rarely find them and when I do they are taking an exam or I am teaching something out of my certification.

Also, just last night *I had a dream that I robbed a bank. I had a gun and I actually shot the gun over everyone's head into a window because I wanted to see if I could get the bullet to go through that window and into the next window that I saw. I was with two other girls, one being an old roommate by name but it didn't look like her. I was sitting on top of the counter while the tellers loaded the money and I looked over the counter and saw a bunch of quarters and I grabbed a handful and said that I would take these too. We took off running in different directions and I ran into a building to hide and saw the police drive by. I causally went to the window and said there must have been an accident. I didn't have the money on me and wasn't sure who did but I looked out of the window again and my friend had taken the bank truck and added sirens to it and was being chased by the police. I woke up before I could find out what happened to the money.*

These two dreams are two of my milder dreams. I can also change what is happening in my dreams if I don't like what is going on. Once I jumped into a pool and a shark bit me and I was aware that it was a dream and so I changed it and the sharks were gone and I jumped back into the pool and swam.

Thanks, FF, female

138

Response

The college dream is highlighting the higher learning available to you in life that is being missed. Controlling your dreams – changing the theme, scene, characters is a refined skill not recommended for beginners. The reason why is that when you change something like killing your sharks you are actually changing thought energies in the inner levels of your consciousness. You may not like the sharks in your dream but that is a poor replacement for understanding what those sharks represent to you and the way you think. Being teachers, we have had occasions to hear many tales of dream-changes that then presented the dreamer with conditions s/he had to respond to. Learn first. Then control. Think of it as driving a car. Learn the steps of how the car works and how to wield it, practice, then drive. It's safer than just getting in, turning it on and going.

The bank dream is talking about value that you haven't earned. You desire to cause a change in your own understanding of this but it is your practice to purposefully take the easy way. Your dream points out the fallacy in this way of thinking because avoiding discipline leads to lying which in turn leads to losing what self-value you have.

Maybe someone gave you a compliment but you don't believe it's true because you're unaware of how you are that way. You don't see how you've earned it. Or maybe you took credit for something you didn't deserve. Whatever went on during your day, it did not add to yourself and your subconscious mind is telling you how and why. It's an informative dream that can spare you much heartache if you'll heed its message.

139

"*Death Passed me By*"

Our local newspaper wrote that your weekend of dream hotline activity was THIS weekend!!! But I see your website says it was LAST weekend. Oh well...

Forty or so years ago I dreamed

I was walking in a heavy forest, going up trail on slight slope through trees. Heard haunting strains of stringed instrument from afar. Saw in distance coming down trail toward me white or pale gray horse walking BACKWARDS (rump toward me as he progressed), with rider sitting backwards so he was facing me in same direction horse was progressing. Rider was tall and cloaked and hooded, playing ancient lute or similar instrument. As they came closer I stepped off the trail to give them passage. As they passed I looked up and saw that rider was skeleton with head half bone & half flesh, with dry long straight gray hair on only one-half of head, and his fleshless fingers slowly strummed his stringed instrument. He didn't look at me, just straight in front of him, as they faded into the distance. He also had no eyes, only sockets. Shortly after that, I was in very severe life-threatening auto accident. I've always figures Death missed me.

I've thought of writing a book -- each chapter one of my marvelous dreams. (Many of them kept in journal and all of them indelible in my mind for years.) I used to have MANY near-astral--projection phenomenal out-of-body experiences in the form of near-sleep or dreams. Miss them. (I'm in 60s and no longer so active n my mind, apparently -- am settled and basically content.) Would like to reactivate that part of my subconscious. Any comments?

THANK YOU

Response

At the time of your dream you were relying heavily upon your inner self, living in the subconscious mind. Your will power was directed by an unknown subconscious aspect that was incomplete, not able to see where you were going. It was not precognitive in the sense that it foretold the wreck, but it did reveal your need to fulfill your purpose for life. I'm not sure how the accident changed your life, but you know and that's what matters.

If this was a current dream without serious investigation it might be difficult to tell the import of it. Hindsight in this case is definitely 20/20. But had you been recording your dreams for a few years, this dream would probably have stood out as different from the rest, or the earlier dreams might have helped you make the adjustments in thinking so this dream might never have been. The important thing is you survived and have much to offer now because of the life you've lived.

Curiosity is a key for you. Teaching others will help rekindle your subconscious connection. Writing a book would enable you to assimilate your experiences and thus enrich your command of them. It's like having a cup that's full, you need to pour some out to have space to receive. Whether it is published for a wide audience or is a personal tome, the act of thinking and writing itself will be your reward for it will help shape the person you are becoming in your every day life.

BOOKSTORE

I was with a couple of friends at a local bookstore chain trying to find a gift for a friend of mine. As we searched through the piles, I noticed a friend of mine was standing beside the large line at the checkout counter. I asked him why he was there and he said that he had been arrested for pushing his buggy through the line up and people complained that he was butting. They were waiting for mall security to come. I told him to tell security that I was his older sister (I am 2 years older than him) and that our parents are out of town and because I'm of legal age, I should be considered a temporary guardian, this way his family will never know. I told him to take out his driver's license so I could memorize his address in case they tried to verify what I said.

The dream then switched to me at the book table. We found a book on India and we were all saying how much our other friend would like it. But then it occurred to me that we were shopping for the wrong person. I told them Maria (the one who's birthday we were shopping for) wouldn't want the book and that we were really thinking of this other girl who's actually Indian and would want it.

We laughed about our mistake and that's where it ended.

C, female

Response

You are aware of a tremendous amount of information available to you. You were searching for specific information that would help you fulfill a subconscious aspect of your Self as represented by your male friend. There is a need for subconscious discipline. Through the course of your actions and consciousness you become dishonest with what you know from experience, with your own inner authority symbolized by parents and security guards.

Through the dishonesty you become confused and lose clarity as to what part of you actually needs the information. What you desire is permanent, not temporary. Information is temporary knowledge, it gains permanence by incorporating it into your thinking and therefore your life experiences. Your dream is telling you, you need to go beyond gathering information and start feeding your subconscious mind understandings.

As a place to begin, it will be good for you to practice honesty and become fully aware of times when you know what is the best thing to do and you do something else. By doing what is right you will begin using your life experiences more fully thus accelerating your soul progression through new understandings.

Tidal Waves & Rivers

I have had recurring dreams about water for just about
my whole life. Previously it was always about tidal
waves and feeling so helpless when I would look up and
see a huge wave coming. Recently, It has been more
about rivers and contained water like in pools surround-
ing houses or hotels. I'm always trapped in some way by
the water and in some danger, although I never drown in
the dreams, I was just saying the other day that I wished
I could find someone who could explain the significance
of these dreams so that I could understand what my
subconscious is trying to tell me about my life. I hope
maybe someone there can help--thank you.
MB, female

Response

Dreams are messages from your subconscious mind relating to your conscious mind your state of consciousness
during the previous 24 hours. Reoccurring dreams indicate
that your subconscious mind is trying repeatedly to "get
your attention" about a certain topic in your life. Water in
a dream represents your conscious, waking experiences.
Your dreams of water are showing you how you have
related to your experiences during the day. Your dreams in
the past of tidal waves and feeling helpless show that this
is the way the you felt about the experiences in your life.
The more recent dreams show that you felt restricted by
your experiences in your life. Overall there is a sense of
helplessness, as if you believe there are many situations in
your life that you can do nothing about. It would be helpful
to realize, practice, and live the truth that you always have
choices and options. When you are able to do this, then you
will have dreams of swimming in a beautiful ocean.

PUZZLING 'RELATIVE' DREAM

I had this puzzling dream last night and it involved my deceased grandfather, who has appeared in about 4-6 dreams in the last 25 years, my brothers who are on good terms, but live in different states and haven't seen each other in 3 years, my husband and my mother.

I dreamed that we were going to a large hall to hear a speaker on wildlife and he was going to do a book signing. It was held in a room just like the one at Hotel Roanoke, but we were apparently in Richmond. David (my husband) and I were there and found our seat up front (left side) early. Then I looked up and saw (brother) Jim. Jim was dressed in outdoorsy type clothes, like (Jim) had just come in from checking alligator nests with the speaker. I yelled to him(we were in a room with 800 people) and he looked happy to see us and came over and sat with us. In the meantime, David had found (brother) Steve and gotten him a seat and I turned around and there was Grandpa. He came up and was so happy to see us all! He was patting Jim on the back and shaking hands with Steve across the table. I thought he seemed a little shaky, though. But he looked happy. Then I went outside for some-

thing and ran into mom in the parking lot. It was a really pretty day and we were dressed in light summery clothes. Mom said she wasn't going in; she had something else to do and I said Jim, Steve, David and Grandpa are in there and she said she hoped we'd have a good visit and she'd see us later.

That's pretty much it. I wondered if Grandpa was shaky because he's preparing me that he won't be 'visiting' me much in the future. He's appeared in times of stress or once to warn me about an accident that surely would've been fatal and his appearance saved me. But in the last several years, when I've really needed him, he hasn't been in my dreams....nothing I do can bring him to my dreams either. He was a father figure for me in real life (even though my father is alive).
Thanks for your help.

AW, female

Response

In every dream every night is a message about your conscious awareness. Everyone and everything in your dream represents a part of you. Your subconscious mind uses the people, places and things familiar to you to convey its message. What these people, places and things symbolize to you is the interpretation of that message.

Your dream indicates you are looking for universal ideas that are compulsive ways of thinking. This could be anything from trying to gain information about shared belief systems (be it believing there is a God or the recent Y2K scare) to ideas that doctors can cure, heal, or always know best or that good always triumphs over evil. You will have to remember what you were thinking and dealing with the day before the dream in order for it to make sense to you in your life.

At any rate, the important subconscious aspects (the male relatives) of yourself are involved in this endeavor, trying to fulfill your desire to understand. One, symbolized by Jim, pushes you toward your goal. Determine which subconscious aspect of you he represents and you will have one of the keys to this message. The second key is in Grandpa. He is in your dream because he represents how you see your superconscious mind. In fact, he symbolizes a way you used to view your own inner authority that has changed (because in physical life Grandpa has passed away) but you still hold onto. Again old beliefs, old habits in the thinking.

The dream even tells you how you can bring yourself into the present through the final action with your mother. She is the receptive aspect of your superconscious mind that is not concerned with the old ways. Aligning yourself with this openness to your own inner authority is what you are ready for. The School of Metaphysics teaches this alignment through transcendent meditation beginning with the cultivation of the still mind. Check out *meditation* at www.som.org

BRAIN TUMOR

I just read an article on your organization in my morning Sunday paper. What caught my eye was that it was very coincidental to two very vivid disturbing dreams I had the previous (Sat.) night and I was thinking about them, trying to decipher their meaning. Maybe you and your staff can provide some additional insight.

The First Dream:

I had been diagnosed with a brain tumor and had been given only a short time to live. I remember getting a second and third medical opinions to be sure. I spent the rest of the dream performing two actions, one: my best to show love understanding, and compassion to those closest to me (my wife, children, & extended Family (parents, brothers & sister)) knowing that they would be deeply saddened by my demise. two: me trying to appreciate to the fullest my life and all the blessings I had received during my life. I remember feeling frightened about my impending death and somewhat insecure.

I forced my self to wake up so that I could end the dream and avoid that feeling. Upon reflecting on that dream this morning, two ideas came to mind, one: I had taken a severe fall three years ago and fractured (& bruised my brain) my skull. This was brought on by my overindulgence of too much alcohol during a visit from one of my brothers from out of town. During my recovery I very much felt guilt in what I was putting my family through, and my lack of responsibility. I asked God's help for a full recovery and made a covenant with him to never drink alcohol again. To this date I have kept that promise! I can definitely say that my life has benefited from that promise, professionally, personally, and spiritually. It came to mind that I might still be feeling guilt resulting from my irresponsibility causing the fall or God may be warning me have the injury rechecked.

Dream two:

I was having a standard business day when I noticed these jellyfish like creatures floating through the air outside of my window. They were jellyfish like in appearance with long tentacles trailing underneath them. I turned on the radio and heard the emergency broadcast system stating that the earth was being invaded and to stay indoors. According to the announcer, if the aliens stung you with one of their tentacles you became their servant and would follow their instructions. The people who became their servants were dragging people who had not been stung yet, into the streets so that the aliens could sting them and enslave them also. The radio announcer was saying that there were millions of these creatures attacking all nations of the earth simultaneously. The announcer stated that no one as of yet knew how to stop them. I have an office in my home so I was personally safe. However, I was concerned about my wife and children who were at work and school respectively. I didn't know how I was going to reach them to help protect them without exposing myself to their sting. I spent the whole dream running from building to another running from the aliens and the people who had become their slaves, trying not to become a slave myself. I wanted desperately to find my family and to protect them. I forced myself to wake up at least four times trying to end this dream, but every time I went back to sleep I would reenter the dream at the point where I had previously left off. I remember explicit details of the entire dream. I remember at the end feeling almost trapped, alone, and desperate.

What is your staff's take on these dreams, especially two so vivid in detail in the same night!

DLH, male

Response

During the day of your dream a negative thinking pattern symbolized by the brain tumor took over your consciousness. A pattern that was going to change (death) you. You knew you needed healing (medical opinions) and you started striving to do better, seeking to unite and harmonize. Realizing this "bad attitude" even stimulated you to begin acknowledging your assets, being grateful for the good things in yourself and your life. Even so, you were still unsettled with what change was coming about from the negativity.

Dreams are symbolic so it's unlikely you need to have the old head injury examined, but if it will ease your mind, do so. There may be greater truth to the connection you saw between the dream and your feelings of guilt. You may have been feeling guilty as you have been becoming more aware of how responsible you truly are for your thoughts and actions. In fact guilt may well be the negative thinking pattern referred to in your dream.

Your second dream reveals how you are at the mercy of other peoples' thoughts. This message is so important to you that it continues through four interruptions. This is a dream about habitual thoughts that are destructive to you. They are also alien, meaning they are foreign to your way of thinking. These are telepathic thoughts symbolized by the EBS on radio. These "alien" thoughts are victim thoughts (I can't, You won't, etc.) that are affecting more and more parts of your existence. You want to take control of yourself, thinking for yourself, but you don't know how.

You need to begin studying metaphysics at SOM. You are ready for a change and you want to take control of your life. This begins with knowing and directing your thoughts through concentration, memory development, and visualization. The thoughts you receive from others are neutral, you determine their direction in your life through awareness and will power. With knowledge there is nothing to fear. We are all connected. Learning Self-control and Self-discipline is the first step to remaining free and responsible for Self and to others.

Call the school nearest you (www.som.org) or headquarters 417-345-8411, so you can start today.

Cute little puppies

I had a night of the same dream over and over. I dreamt of finding cute little puppies of different breeds. I was picking them up and feeling so happy to be finding them.
They were very cuddly.

I would wake up after and when I fell asleep again I would dream the same dream again. I had this same dream at least three times in one night. Does this mean anything?

CM,female

Response

Animals in a dream represent habits. Even cute little puppies. In fact your enjoyment and the continuity of the dream both indicate that these habits are ones you like. You will need to determine what habit your subconscious mind is talking about. It could mean something good like a habit of making people feel at home and therefore comfortable, or it could mean something not so good like a habit of taking perscribed drugs because it makes you feel better. The important thing is that your subconscious mind is letting you know the state of your conscious awareness.

The PSYCHIC MAN

I had a dream that i went to talk to this psychic man (i have talked to him in real life before). He was talking to me and said that i had two best friends (which is true) and that one of them is brain dead (one of my best friends i don't really like) then the psychic man went on to tell me that I was married to a guy named Justin. (i have liked this guy for a while but just recently gotten over him, we are still friends) then in my dream i had a vision of Justin and i in a horse drawn carriage and i had a wedding dress on etc. it was like we had just been married. we were laughing and looked as though we were very happy.

what does this dream mean I'm so confused. thank you for your time
LM, female

Response

All dreams are about the dreamer. People in a dream represent aspects of the dreamer. This dream is about your desire to know the future symbolized by the psychic man who represents your capacity for subconscious clairvoyance. Your dream is telling you that you have been examining the aspects that you have and have identified productive ones (*Justin*) and unproductive ones (*brain dead friend*). You have made a commitment (*marriage*) to use the productive ones to direct your life (*horse drawn carriage*). Your wise choice, pleases you.

RATTLESNAKE!

I remembered only parts of this dream but thought it would be interesting to see what you think.

Someone (a male, but I don't remember who) is holding me up off the ground so that a rattlesnake doesn't bite me. There doesn't seem to be any concern on my part or the part of the person holding me that they could get bit too. Not sure how it happened but I ended up getting bit while the person was still holding me. I got bit on the left ankle/foot area. Then there were some moments where no one believed that I had been bit. I was trying to convince everyone but since at the time there was no mark nobody was believing me. Then the red streak that you get from being bitten appeared and people started to believe me. I remember thinking I have to get help before the streak of poison makes it up to my heart.

Then I remember leaving to drive myself to the hospital but first I stopped off to pick up lunch for the people I work with. Inside the restaurant the order was either not ready or wrong and I became very angry and started yelling at the manager. He was mean back and yelled at me. Then I followed him into the back room I became tearful and apologized and explained what had just happened with the snake and why I was in such a hurry. All the time this was happening I was very mindful that the streak was moving closer to my heart. The I remember being in a hospital bed and some male (uniden-

tified) was lying the in bed with me to offer comfort
and support. He was only there for a moment. Then
my parents show up at the side of the hospital bed.
My Dad is quiet and very serious looking, my Mom
is crying. I remember thinking that I was going to
be okay since I was in the hospital. I was feeling
fairly calm despite the fact that the streak of poison
had made it to just under my breast bone.
Then I woke up.

MI, female

Response

This dream is about love and creativity. You relied on
your subconscious mind rather than gaining conscious
wisdom the day of this dream. You needed to be
creative in how you will move forward in your life, for
instance the next step to take toward a desired goal.
You are motivated to change (fear of death) by force
rather than by love (heart). When forced to, you will
take control of your mind and your body, even gain the
knowledge you lack. You will also open yourself to
healing. Once you start creating you realize how much
you love it. How much it creates an alignment in you,
consciously, subconsciously and superconsciously as
symbolized by the male and your parents respectively.
When that streak reaches your heart you will know
you are free from being forced to change because you
can now change from love and desire. This is a great
dream even if it probably was a bit scary to your
conscious mind.

DEAD PEOPLE

I dream about dead people over and over. They all seem to be my mother, grandparents and elderly friends. Mostly women who were close to me growing up. I have happen to be with a few of them when they died. Is it because I miss them? Some of my grandparents and I didn't have that great of relationships. But the other people and I did. They usually tell me they are all right, but I wake myself up crying usually. What does this all mean?

F&N, female

Response

There are two basic rules about dreams. These will aid you to identify what the dream message is communicating to you. First, everyone in your dream is you. Secondly, everything in the dream is about you. All dreams describe your state of awareness. Therefore, you will want to interpret each one symbolically as having meaning for you.

It is also possible for loved ones to communicate to you while in the dreamstate. When this is occurring the loved ones will have their mouths closed and you will still be receiving communication or you simply might hear them but not see them in the dream.

The aspects in this dream are aspects of yourself. The fact that they are mostly people who have authority represents your higher self. This is known as the superconscious mind. It is the "Jiminy Cricket" part of yourself. It knows right from wrong and serves as our inner urge to be like our Creator. These people in your dream have died. Death symbolizes change. In other words, you have caused a change in how you view your higher self and how you relate to your higher self. There is a need to trust this change and remember that you have already caused this change. Let go of the old way and your pain will cease.

Riding Bicycles

My recurring dream is one of me *riding one of those old fashioned bicycles, the kind with the front wheel much larger than the rear one. I am sitting way up on it, and can actually feel what it would be like to ride it. The handle bars are small and close to me. I am riding looking for someplace to stop to park, someplace where I can lean it since I am so high up on it. I'm having a hard time finding a light pole or someplace to stop so I can get off.* If I believed in reincarnation, I would swear that I rode a bicycle like this in an earlier life, but that goes against all my beliefs. Please interpret.

MC, female

Response

This dream is talking about balance. Much more than juggling physical activity so everything has equal time, balance is the use of the aggressive and receptive actions of mind together. You are looking for awareness so you can still in your mind. This will give you the control you are looking for to get off the bike at will.

Molestation

My daughter came to me and told me that she is having a reoccurring dream. Her father and I are currently going through a divorce after 21 years and she is 18 years old with a new baby herself.

She told me that she has a dream where her father is trying to molest her...the next night she has a dream where my current boyfriend is trying to molest her. Now I know she is torn between the two men. She loves her father but she also cares for my new boyfriend. Can you please give us some advice on what these dreams could mean to her. Thank you very much....

Response

A reoccurring dream shows how a person is repeating a pattern of thinking. This dream has to do with how your daughter uses her own mind to create (sexual activity). Although it may seem that this dream is literal, it really represents her own relationship with herself. Her father represents her superconscious mind, her own inner authority, and your new boyfriend is a quality of her inner self or subconscious mind. She thinks that creation is being forced on her.

When your daughter identifies what she wants to create she will experience greater inner cooperation toward the fulfillment of that ideal. This dream is easily understood when put in the context of being young with a baby of her own. Setting goals for herself is essential for her mental and physical health. Visualization will aid her, and meditation will help her to know and harmonize with her inner self. Then creation can become a natural, an easy, joyful part of life.

Baby Dreams

I am curious as to what a reoccurring dream would be where I have a baby and I am all alone and have nothing for the baby. And here recently I've been dreaming about having my tubes tied and I haven't even had a child yet. Can you tell me what this means?

Thank you for your time and I look forward to your response.

KH, female

Response

Every dream is important and gives you awareness of your daily conscious thinking. Having a baby in a dream is how you are creating a new idea or way of life. Yet you think you don't have the ability to respond to it or nurture it to grow. The way to cause a new idea to grow is to give this part of you positive attention, to visualize how you want to be, and to then learn and grow with it.

The second dream of having your tubes tied represents how you cut off your ability to create something new in your life. The ability to create is inherent in each of us. As you accept this truth and cooperate with your own inner and outer mind, you'll be able to have what you desire in your life.

Back with the person she's
DIVORCING

I am in the process of a divorce, been separated 18
months, have had to do court battles, because he physically abused me for years, before i finally left. had to
fight him in court for custody or our son. this man has
been nothing but rotten to both my son and i, after 18
months, i still can not get our belongings out of the
house.

Keep having a dream where I'm back in his house,
kinda like dating. he will be Mr. nice guy one minute
and then go pick up his girlfriend and bring her over
there with my son and i. last night i dreamt that i was
there and all i remember was having tears in my eyes,
and him saying to me, just lay your head on my shoulder.

I thought i was getting my life back together, but
recently all these dreams leave me confused and agi-
tated.

Help please

Response
Every dream is about the dreamer, and every person,
place and thing in the dream represents a part of the
dreamer. So this dream is not about your husband! It
is about your relationship with your inner self. The
need that it brings to your attention is a need to fulfill
your commitments to yourself, and this will bring you
the security and clarity you desire.

Family Gathering

Our relatives are all gathering together like a funeral, everybody asks my sister where i am she tells them I'm in the back room. My sister and my dad go into a room and there i am laying in bed with a brand new baby.

I am 45 years old. With two boy's 12 and 10 years old. I am overweight and trying to lose weight. Christian single parent raising my boys on my own.

WP, female

Response

A simple dream with a simple but life-changing message. The aspects of yourself that you are most familiar with are acknowledging a change that has occurred which turns out to be a new idea you have created. You will need to put it into your life. It could be anything from joining a weight loss group and then coming up with the idea you can do it on your own to the new way of life initiated by the change in your family structure following a divorce. It's your dream, only you can say.

MY OWN DEATH

Hello. I have two dreams I'd like to tell you about.
Please tell me what you think about them.

I am a 26 year old female, mother of one, from the
Midwest. *Twice in my life I've dreamt of my death.
In the one I remember really well, I have one child
(at the time of the dream, I wasn't pregnant, married, engaged, or seeing anyone and had no children) and I am really really sick. I am dying from
some disease (cancer? I don't know) that is making
me very thin and very weak (at the time of the
dream, I was a heavy woman). I went with my
parents, sisters, my child and my mother's sister &
her husband to pick out my casket. This all seemed
very natural.*

Also:
*In December 1995, I had a dream that seemed to
last a lifetime: I dreamed I met and married a
wonderful man. I got pregnant and had a wonderful
baby girl. I dreamed about her until right before her
third birthday and then I awoke. What is so weird to
me about this dream, is that unlike any I've had
before and any I've had since, in the dream I went
through the courtship, engagement, wedding,
pregnancy, birth and the child's first two years DAY
by DAY in the dream. There wasn't any skipping
around.*

Response

Dreams are always symbolic. Death in a dream indicates change. In the first dream you have a new idea. You are aware of an unproductive attitude which is causing a weak mind. The change you are preparing to make is the result of an unproductive attitude. There is a need to strengthen your ideals to produce something, rather than changing because you have to. The dream indicates there is no other choice but to change.

The second dream shows the progression you have gone through as a result of making a commitment to the self. First you recognize a part of your inner self that you like and decide to make a commitment with this part of the inner self. You begin to create with this part of the self which produces a new idea. Each dream tells the state of awareness. This is why the dream stops where it does. You have reached the point where the new idea is starting to flourish on its on.

MY RE-OCCURRING DREAM

IN THIS DREAM I AM YOUNG ABOUT TEN YEARS OLD, I'M IN A HOTEL WITH SMALL DOORS AND STAIRS LEADING TO LITTLE ELEVATORS, BUT THE ELEVATORS ARE JUST BOXES WITH STRINGS ATTACHED TO THE TOP. I RUN UP AND DOWN DIFFERENT CURVED, STRAIGHT, AND CROOKED STAIRS UNTIL THERE IS NO WHERE ELSE TO RUN BUT THERE IS ONE LAST ELEVATOR-BOX THING, IT DOESN'T LOOK SAFE BUT THERE IS SOMEONE FOLLOWING ME AND I HAVE TO GO IN OR THE PERSON-THING FOLLOW-ING ME WILL CATCH ME. I NEVER CAN SEE WHAT IS FOLLOWING ME BUT I STEP INTO THIS BOX AND AS I AM CLIMBING IN THE BOX IT STARTS TO FALL AND THEN I WAKE UP.

THIS DREAM HAS HAUNTED ME SINCE I WAS ABOUT FIFTEEN. IF YOU HAVE ANY AN-SWERS AS TO WHY I HAVE THIS DREAM PLEASE WRITE ME BACK.
THANKS,

VM, female

164

Response

You do not say your current age, but from what you do say this dream began when you were 15 years old. This is important because it is a dream from adolescence.

At the time this dream occurs you are seeing yourself as more immature, less experienced than you really are. The immaturity revolves around your understanding of the difference between imaging and pretending. You are seeking universal truth – what we call the principles of visualization in the School of Metaphysics – and not finding anything that is real. This becomes a limitation to you because you don't have the answers you feel you need or are ready for. So you do the best with what you have. You feel forced to experience.

This quality is often reflected in dreamers from 10 to 20. It is only in the recent years that knowledge about consciousness and what is beyond the physical world is becoming available. Eventually it is our hope that this will become part of the parental and educational system teachings. It is important to know what the mind is, how it functions and why, and how to direct it responsibly. You are seeking this knowledge, particularly about the power of your mind to create. Read **Shaping Your Life** at www.som.org as a first step.

No matter how old you are physically when this dream comes to you, it is telling you about a young frame of mind you have been carrying around since the age of 15. Solve the dream message and the dream will stop and new dreams will take its place.

By the way, the falling elevator simply represents your consciousness moving from the sleep to the waking state.

Stranger in *my* Bed

I am sleeping in my old room at my parents'
house. In bed with me is my sister. She was hot so
she threw off the covers and I was cold so I put
them back on us. After a little debate we came to
a resolution, she would keep the covers off on her
and I would keep them on me. We went to sleep. I
woke up in the middle of the night because I had
to go to the bathroom. I looked over at my sister
and noticed that it wasn't her lying next to me. I
looked more closely and notice that this person
was a man with long gray shoulder length hair. I
touched this person just to make sure that it was
my sister and it wasn't.

A sense of fear came over me, all I know is
that I had to leave quickly. As I was getting out of
the bed, this man asked me where I was going and
that I couldn't leave. I looked at his face more
closely and noticed that this person lying next to
me was old (80 years or more) and his voice was
very deep. He spoke to me saying that I could not
leave this room. Then he grabbed me and pulled
down on the bed, his grip getting tighter on my
arms. I remember waking up Yelling "NO, NO"
feeling my heart beating faster. I remember lying
in bed calming my self down.

DW, female, CA

Response

This dream reveals that the day before, you had been thinking in an old way, a familiar way. You were having a struggle with a conscious aspect of yourself, very familiar. The struggle was something having to do with being expansive or reflective (hot and cold) in your thinking. You came to what you thought was a resolution so you could rest and assimilate.

You recognized a need to release unproductive thoughts (*the bathroom*) but in the process, you soon experienced feeling trapped, though, by some way you were experiencing your subconscious thoughts. You were thinking more and more about the issue, trying to come to wisdom, but in the process trapped yourself in the thoughts, trying to understand the purpose of it all. You were feeling "stuck", or boxed in. You've thought a lot about it, but not acted yet.

Your panic at the end of the dream was a response in your conscious mind to feeling trapped in the thoughts and thinking, as you woke up. Please let us know how we can serve you further, or if you have more questions.

Losing Teeth

This is the second time I have dreamt of losing teeth. The first dream was about 2 months ago but I distinctly remember it. However, last night I had another that was worse than the first time.

I was home or rather another house that I used to live in a while ago. I felt one of my teeth felt loose and I wiggled it with my tongue like I remember doing as a kid. I felt the suction of the gums trying to hold the tooth in but it wiggled free. I could feel the hole in my gum and taste the metallic blood taste. But, as I spit out the one tooth I discovered that I spit out more than one tooth. I felt as if my entire mouth was full of loose teeth and to make myself believe it I spit into my hand and saw my teeth. My front teeth, back teeth..all of them without a drop of blood on them...but I could taste the blood in my mouth and feel the tender gums with my tongue.

In the dream I remembered the previous dream and at some point realized I was dreaming...I was trying to understand why in the first dream I had only lost one tooth and now I was losing them all. Then I woke up and it felt so real that I actually had to make sure it was a dream.

A, female

Response

Dreaming of your teeth falling out is very common. Your dreams reflect back to you your conscious state of awareness during the previous 24 hours. Both of these dreams are speaking to you about the way that you assimilate knowledge. Since food in a dream represents knowledge, your teeth symbolize the means by which you receive that knowledge. In the second dream being in an old house symbolizes your mind. It shows that you were thinking in an old, if very familiar, way. This dream is telling you that the way you used to receive knowledge will no longer work for you in the present. You need new tools to assimilate. This may mean learning a new skill like computer programming or competitive swimming or concentration and visualization. As your mind expands, old ways of learning will be outgrown and new ways brought under your command.

Terrorists

in one of my dreams, *i was in a mall that was being infiltrated by terrorists who were trying to get inside. there was a swat team with helicopters trying to stop them. i was taken hostage. one of the male terrorists accidentally shot another, who was an African female. lots of gunfire ensued afterward. the girl and i escaped inside. i tried to warn everyone of what was going on outside, but no one took me seriously. the terrorists finally got in, and they began attacking the civilians. several of the male terrorists began gang raping the male civilians. i hid in a corner and just saw everything happening.*

i am a 21 year old female from CA.

Response

This dream is all about the your destructive ways of thinking taking over your mind. The terrorists represent aspects of you that are causing fear, destruction, and forced change. You attempt to control your Self through all the discipline you can muster, yet this does not stop these aspects of destruction from invading your mind. The biggest destructive force is conscious doubt. There is also a need for you to take activity towards your needs and desires. By assuming conscious responsibility for how you think you will begin to determine the world you live in.

Find a way to strengthen your concentration abilities and gain awareness of your thoughts. Journaling every day will help you to still your mind and see your thoughts written in front of you. Your thoughts create your world and show up in your dreams. The more you change your thoughts to productive thinking of what you desire and who you want to become, the more joyful changes you will experience.

Puzzle Dreams

I have re-occurring dreams (not the same dream) where I am trying to figure out or solve a problem or puzzle. Sometimes they are so intense they wake me up. Not sure what this means. In my job I solve computer problems -- my dreams are not about computer problems.

Thanks

BL, female

Response

The dreams you have reflect your thoughts and attitudes of the previous day or couple of days. If you constantly dream of problem solving, it means that your mind is constantly in motion, reaching to come to conclusions. The fact that this wakes you up means that your mind is working too aggressively. Whether solving a problem or creating a masterpiece, you need to be aggressive and receptive. Receptivity requires a still mind. With a still mind, answers come.

The best way to use these two qualities is to use your mind to 'aggressively' reach for an answer. When reaching becomes painful or uncomfortable, then you stop and go do something else for a while, all the while expecting that you will come to a conclusion. (sleep on it, if you will) This is receptive! Many times the answers come in a seemingly effortless manner.

Those are the aggressive and receptive principles at work!!

Escape from Danger

I was just wondering what it means when u dream about flying? I usually have dreams where I'm flying way from danger i.e someone trying to kill me.

Response

Flying in a dream indicates that during the day previous to having the dream you experienced a sense of freedom in your life. Dreams always reflect your state of consciousness, so look at the days previous to having flying dreams and ask yourself how you were creating and experiencing freedom during that day. Understanding how you created freedom in your life will then enable you to reproduce it.

Death in a dream indicates change so on the days when you dream that you are running away from someone trying to kill you, ask yourself if there is some change in your life that you are avoiding. Answering these two questions, "how do I create freedom" and "what changes am I avoiding" will aid you to use the messages being conveyed to you in these dreams.

SPIRITS

I had a dream last year that my husband passed
away and I had no idea what to do. He means a lot
to me and I do not want to lose him. We have been
married for 2 years and I was just wondering what
that had meant.

Since then I have read a book about spirits and
I have been ok. Although, I do jump sometimes
when I am sleeping . I have been doing this since I
was like 16. I will just lay there and sleep and then
all of a sudden my body will just jump really quick
and it wakes me up. I never have a dream that I am
falling or anything it is really weird. I was just
wondering if any of this meant anything.

Thank you! Megan from Alaska

Response

The dream of your husband passing away is a message about
commitment to creating wholeness within yourself. Your
husband is a symbol of an inner aspect of your subconscious
mind (male), committed to creating wholeness (marriage)
within yourself. Passing away/death means a change has
occurred in your subconscious mind. This most probably
means you have gained an understanding since understood
experiences are stored by the soul, the "brain" of subconscious mind.

Awakening from a sudden "jump" in the physical body
is indicating that your attention is snapped back to your
physical body when you are trying to relax into the inner
levels. This could be from an external stimulus like a loud
noise or from an internal one like fear. Developing your
concentration skills by practicing concentration exercises
daily will stop this from occurring.

The *ADDAMS FAMILY*

I have had two reoccurring dreams for years – almost 10 – in the first one

I am being chased, by different people, some times it has been soldiers, regular people, etc. It also takes place in different places, my home, a church, the woods, a warehouse. I am never caught by anyone. In some I just run, in others I pick up a gun but can't get the safety off, there may be no bullets, or it will fire once and then misfire. Sometimes I just keep running. Then I wake up.

The second one *I haven't had in a while since a pivotal moment in the last one but I thought you may be interested because I had this dream at very regular intervals for several years also. I lived in what was at one time a beautiful Victorian mansion, but it was run down like something in the Addams Family! But the strange thing was I could only live in a few rooms because the others were haunted. Furniture flying around in some of the rooms and some I just didn't go in because of the fact that they were haunted by someone and just too creepy. But the rooms I lived in were fine, sunny (but dusty). I would open the doors into the haunted rooms - sometimes by myself and sometimes I'd show someone. This house was huge also --different wings and separate levels. I would go back through the same places in different dreams-- there was one that was upstairs, a huge one down a dark, long hall; a balcony; a basement; a hidden stairway that led to the attic. Just a huge, sprawling place but I could only inhabit a couple of rooms. Anyway, I finally -- after opening the door several times and shutting it back- went in to the attic where I had a fight with the Devil. I won, and have never had the dream again.*

The strange thing is I moved in to another house that wasn't as nice, still haunted by spirits that liked to turn the lights off and leave me in the dark.

I only had that dream a few times though and it has been a while since I had a "house" dream. I was chased again last night and saw an article in the paper on your school, I thought maybe you would have some insight.

Thank you
SM, female, VA

Response

Being chased in a dream indicates you are avoiding aspects and qualities of your Self. Trying to use the gun shows a desire for change that you put effort towards. You are still not able to cause the change and there is still the need to face your fears and what you are avoiding.

In Dream 2, the house represents the condition of your mind. The house being large and run down shows you have vast potential in your mind, but you are not responding to it. You limit how you can use your mind. Developing an adventurous attitude of curiosity and learning to interpret your dreams will help you to overcome your fears.

The devil represents your conscious ego. By "winning" you conquered your conscious ego that day. You now see your mind differently, and have a tendency to ignore what is going on. The above suggestions will help.

Trucking Accidents...

I read the 25 most common dream symbols, but still wonder. I have two (2) reoccurring dreams, perhaps you can give more info.

1. I frequently dream that I will have an accident with a big truck (semi), (I drive a big truck) I have been involved in 4 incidents in the past 5 years. The first, a lady stopped in the driving lane going down a 6 % grade, was unable to avoid, considerable damage to car, people claimed not to be hurt at scene, but later took insurance company to cleaners (one of occupants was Chiropractor's mom!). Second, A lady (drunk) tried to pass on right, loss control, totaled her car, left the scene, was charged DWI, etc. Third, one car towing another on freeway, decided to exit, forgot he was towing and cut in front of my truck, pulling towed car into my truck. Result, minor injuries, two cars totaled! Fourth, a city worker ran a red light, drove under the trailer, roadway was slippery, so vehicle was "kicked" out, instead of being ran over, He received ticket for inattentive driving.

Subsequently, I have had several reoccurring dreams involving cars spinning next to me, trucks going pass my kitchen window (at home on farm where I grew up) crashed into woods, all of which were in vivid color, and I could recognized the make and color of car and see the occupants, In cars, they are always families.

> *2. I am retired from US Army. I frequently dream that I am back in army, (recalled) and have only one uniform and worry constantly that we will have to change to another uniform and I will not have it. And I keep forgetting to buy more uniforms when I am at the clothing store!*

Response

Hi! Thanks for sending us your dreams, it is our privilege to serve. Dreams are a message from the inner self about our waking state and thoughts for the 24 to 48 hours prior to the dream.

All dreams are productive. The first dream reflects how your accidents have affected – and may have been affected by – your state of mind: There is a need to care for your body and cease the recklessness and out-of-control actions of how you use your attention and your body. Being in the kitchen symbolizes that you are already somewhat aware of this, and I suggest you redouble your efforts to use self-control and discipline with your body.

This leads straight into the second set of dreams you gave us for interpretation: The recurring Army dreams show your ability to be disciplined, which is developed and back in current use. You are "recalled back" to needing to be disciplined, and you are concerned that there is only one way (*one uniform*) showing how you can be expressing discipline in your life. Clothing in a dream symbolizes how you appear to others, and you seem to want more ways to express with self control/discipline.

177

Nightmares *of Pain*

My 10 year old has had nightmares for about 3 months now. All have to do with him being hurt physically by weapons. ex. *I'm driving my car he's in the back passenger seat. there was a dead man who was put in the trunk of the car. and he stabbed my child through the seat 2x's. my child remembers the whole nightmare with color.* that really scares me.

every night these nightmares are about him getting stabbed, shot, and it's always him who is getting hurt. please help interpret something to get me started. my child won't even sleep in his room and always wants a light on not a night light either. i want to give him advice but not sure how to; to a 10 year old who's scared half to death of going to bed.

bc

thank you

Response

Every dream relates the individual's conscious state of awareness. Nightmares are a strong message from the inner self that is being ignored, that needs to be listened to. The knife is a tool for change and death in a dream symbolizes change. Your son's dreams indicate he has adopted (or learned) victim consciousness. Change is happening to him rather than him feeling in control of his life. As a parent look and admit what changes are happening around your son. Has he recently moved to another town or school, lost someone he was close to, things of this nature? Ten years of age is a good time to learn how to respond to the unexpected in our lives. Teach him good basic reasoning skills of concentration, memory, listening, visualization, and goal setting. If you feel ill equipped to do so, learn them yourself and then pass them onto your child. He needs you now, not later. (The SOM course teaches these skills, www.som.org)

Encourage your child to share his dreams. Buy **The Dreamer's Dictionary** and use it together. Tell your child his dreams are about himself, and there is nothing to fear. The dead person symbolizes a change that has been made, that your son is still attached to. Look to see what the change was, and help your child to let go of the change and fully make the new change he is attempting currently. Help him live in the present. (Maybe you need to do this also, you can help one another.)

Keep us posted with your progress.

Emergency Room

For about three years I have been having dreams with dead friends and relatives that tell me things that are going to happen . Three years ago I was passing out at work, from stress and awoke in the e.r. and my wife said the I was saying the name Sara, then she asked me who Sara was I said that it was her grandmother. My wife's grandmother name was Sara but always went by Paulina.

In this dream my father, who died in 1977 told me to tell my mother that he misses playing gin with her and that Elvis always cheats. Sara (Paulina) told me that there was something wrong with my sister-in-law Julie's reproductive system, and to tell Mel, my father-in-law that she missed him. Nora a friend that killed herself told me that my wife and I were pregnant, which she was, and then my dad told me that I didn't belong here and that it was time to go home and that's when I awoke in the E.R.

I have had more dreams of this type with Sara, my father, Nora, a person that look like God, and others I don't know if these are dreams or not. My mother calls it the power she says that her mother has this power and also her self and her sister, as well as my sister.
SQC, male

Response

Dreams offer insights into the state of your awareness. When interpreting your dreams there are three universally true principles to keep in mind: 1. Every dream is about the dreamer. 2. Every person, place and thing in the dream represents the dreamer. Dreams are a communication from your inner subconscious mind to your outer conscious mind.

Because they originate in Subconscious Mind, dreams may be precognitive. Such dreams are about probabilities, events that may occur. Additionally, research has revealed that whenever a deceased person visits you in the dream they will relay a message to you without moving their mouth. The message is received telepathically, mind to mind. These dreams can enable you to be prepared and direct your thoughts causing the effect that you desire in possible future events.

These dream experiences could very well be direct communication from loved ones. It could as easily be your own subconscious mind giving you insight, either way the dream is still applicable in your life. To understand this connection, the symbols need to be interpreted.

In your dream your father told you to tell your mother that he misses playing gin and that Elvis cheats. Symbolically your higher self (*dad*) is encouraging a higher purpose to your life. Games in dreams represent the "game" of life. Playing card games well requires reasoning. The part about Julie indicates your need to give your inner, subconscious mind something to recreate for you, in other words you need to be clear about your desires, setting goals that will fulfill them. Nora indicates a response to this need, which is producing a potential for new ways of living (*pregnancy*). Each of these symbols are significant in the dream message.

You might want to spend time reading some of the transcribed lectures at this site (www.dreamschool.org). They have more to say about the many functions of the subconscious mind.

Sweet Dreams!

FIRE

I just want to know what fire symbolizes in a dream? I have recently had a dream that was just full of information, but I do not know what fire represents, and in my dream there was a small fire that really caught my attention and I seemed to focus on this fire.
Please help. Thank you.

Response

One of the five elements in the outer planes, fire symbolizes expansion, the ability to spread out becoming enlarged so as to embrace more.

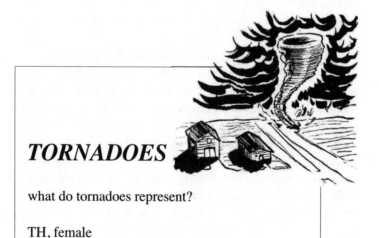

TORNADOES

what do tornadoes represent?

TH, female

Response

Tornadoes represent inner turmoil and confusion.

Dual Tornadoes

I do not remember my dreams typically. But last evening *I had a dream of a tornado heading clearly in a storm for my sister and I as younger people. Then the dream skipped to another tornado siting and this time again we were together but on a large ship again much younger and we or at least I was concerned where our mother was and to get to her to warn or help protect her, this tornado hit the ship with us on it but I have no recollection of the outcome, other than I believe my sister and I were ok-not sure about mother-still had concerns.*

Could you pls. give me an idea what this might be about? It would be appreciated.

Thank YOU PMM

Response

The movement of the tornado in your dreams is reflective of the movement of your waking thoughts; swirling about, moving faster and faster until they become out of control, possibly even destructive.

You identify with yourself as a more immature (younger) you, not recognizing the maturity that you currently have (as symbolized by being younger than you currently are). Within the confusion of your waking life, your dream demonstrates that you are reaching for clarity and seeking your own inner authority. This would be to become rooted in the truth of what you know, of what is right and just.

The need reflected in the dream is to become more directed with your thoughts throughout your day. This will aid you in having clarity of thought and of your Self. Although you have not typically remembered your dreams, you do dream every night. It is important to listen to the messages from your subconscious mind as they will always give you what you need.

Can't Move, Can't Talk

I have a recurring dream that i have had for many many years. The surroundings change as to where i am (in bed, on sofa, in what ever room i am in when I'm asleep) but the dream or nightmare is mostly always the same. It is so real at the time because I know where I'm at and who is present when fall asleep (except once).. It became so real I learned to talk myself out of it, once i realize i am dreaming.

It start where i can not move, talk, or yell and sometimes have trouble breathing. I know where I'm at and how I'm dressed and if I'm in bed for the night or just laying down for a nap. I try to wake up but can't, sometimes I fight to get up and if I do I can't open my eyes and I stumble around until I find myself back on the sofa and realize I did not wake up. Other times i just can't move at all and i fight to get up until I realize what is happening and talk myself into waking up. If it has been sometime between dream I don't always remember right away to talk myself out of it so i might I think I have succeeded in waking up but than throwing back into the paralyzing state several times until I do actually realize what is happening and wake myself up. The only way I ever knew it was a dream my brother was in the house at one of the times i was trying to yell for help (nothing ever comes out) but when I came out of this one i knew he wasn't there.

Basically they are all the same the surroundings is the only thing that changes (whichever home I live in at the time is always my surroundings
female

Response

When we dream we go into the inner levels of mind. What is occurring in your dream is that you are consciously aware of the body, but you are not centered in your body and therefore you can not function. There is an awareness of being awake in the dream state, but you cannot move the body. When this happens you can take in a deep breath. The breath is what ties the soul to the body. Therefore if you take in a breath you will immediately be brought back to the body.

Because there is an awareness you have of the inner levels of mind, I would suggest you follow a structured and disciplined course of study. We offer a course in applied metaphysics which I believe could aid you a great deal. If you would like more information about our course of study, please feel free to call us at (417) 345-8411.

Parents who have passed away....

I heard about you through a friend of mine and, I was interested in knowing what dreams are all about. Here is one of my dreams. *My mom and dad are both deceased. My mom has been gone for 6 years and my dad has been gone for almost 4 years. I have dreams about them all the time. But, this particular dream both of them was in the dream. I never see what my mother has on as far as clothing but, I can see what my dad has on. We were someplace in someone else's house but, the bed that was in the house, it was mine. I don't know what we were talking about but, my dad had just got home and he had no place to sleep so, I got up and I gave him my bed so he can sleep since he had just got off work . My mother never talks to me. We had no conversation at all.*

I don't know what this means but, if you would tell me I would appreciate it.

p.s. I do remember my dad was worried about me because, I had no money and he gave me some.

please respond

thank you   LW, female

Response

In every dream every night is a message about your conscious awareness. Everything and everyone in your dream represents a part of you. You dream every night and the message illustrate the thinking of the previous day.

Dreaming about your parent brings attention to the way you see your own authority. You have authority on something when your knowing comes from your experience. You are using your authority when you share what you know.

In your dream you willingly offered your bed to your father. The day before this dream, you willingly assimilated knowledge. Because your mother is not talking to you, there is a need to learn to be more receptive so further learning can occur.

186

Cannot Sleep

I unfortunately found out about your dream hotline too late to make use of your expertise. I am hoping that someone can answer my questions or point me in the right direction.

For about the last year, I have been having so many vivid dreams each night - they are either very disturbing or nightmarish - that I cannot sleep. This happens on the average 4 nights a week. I feel as if I work so hard in my dreams that I am waking up
Thanks so much,
DB, Female

Response
Dreams are the way the mind assimilates the previous day's experiences. The inner self reflects back to the outer conscious mind our thoughts and attitudes in the form of symbols. A nightmare is a dream designed to get your attention. It indicates there have been messages given repeatedly in dreams that have been ignored or avoided. Knowing this, the subconscious will use something that will be shocking (or sometimes ridiculous) to the waking mind. This grabs your conscious attention and you say you had a nightmare.

You feel exhausted in the morning because the disturbing nature of the dream is affecting your rejuevenation time. Some form of concentration and meditation before bed to calm the mind is in order.

DREAMS? *WHAT DREAMS?*

My wife is always asking me if I had dreams during the previous night's sleep. My answer to her is always the same, "If I had any I don't remember them." She believes that dreams are often times spiritual, and she is looking to me (as the head of the household) to give some kind of spiritual guidance to the family. So why don't I remember my dreams?

MQ, male

Response

There are a number of reasons why people might not remember their dreams. Perhaps they are not that important or interesting to you ! If we wake up in a hurry, we jump from one state of mind to another too quickly to retain the dream experience. When we scatter our attention during the day, it becomes hard to remember our dreams – or anything else for that matter!

If you have a desire to remember your dreams, get a journal for recording them. Before going to sleep, write the next day's date at the top of the page and say to yourself, "I will remember my dreams." Keep the journal by your bed. Another thing that will help is to deliberately give your full attention during the day, to the task at hand or the person talking to you. **The Dreamer's Dictionary** by Barbara Condron is the best book for interpreting your dreams. Buy it and use it every morning. Your life will change for the better!

188

LEAVING MY CHILDREN
UNATTENDED

I have a reoccurring dream that
I leave my children at home alone.
I dream that I'm in work and I look
at my watch and realize that I've
been in work for about an hour and
that I've left my children at home
alone instead of taking them to the
daycare or babysitter's house. Then
I panic and leave work to rush
home to them hoping that they are
okay.

Response

This message is about qualities that you're developing in yourself. They are important to you, but the dream describes a way you drop them from your attention. A way to respond to this dream is to keep these ideas and qualities more in your attention, and imagine ways you can add to them in your daily activities.

A NEW YEAR'S EVE dream...

hello, i am a 21 year old girl from San Diego, CA Here is a dream i had this last new years eve:

i was pregnant. i was homeless, however, so i could not keep my baby. the court said my sister was to have it when it was born. i wanted to take care of it myself. but i was very happy just to be having a baby, so it didn't really bother me that i wasn't able to keep it. i went into labor and was taken to the hospital. i had the baby with no pain, and I felt very happy to be giving birth. when the baby was delivered, it was immediately given to my sister. i sat up and saw her holding my baby in front of me. it was a girl, small but healthy, and she had fair skin, big brown eyes, and lots of brown hair. she was looking right back at me very pleasantly. i was very happy and proud. i just kept gazing at her forever, until i woke up from the dream.

Response

Congratulations! This dream is about a whole new idea of yourself that you have, a whole new way of life you are creating. Since you are homeless in the dream, this idea will change the way you understand yourself. In order to develop this, you will need to imagine how you can build and use and practice this new idea of yourself in your daily activity, and act on your imaged ideal.

This is especially important because your dream indicates the new idea will mature through what the aspect symbolized by your sister represents. Determine which aspect of you your sister is – funny, reliable, stubborn, gregarious, bossy, etc. – and you will understand what this new idea will require from you for its growth and maturity.

190

Roller Coaster Street

Please can you interpret this dream, *I am in my car driving on the expressway extremely fast and to my surprise the street is going straight down & has a drop it's as if I'm on a roller coaster ride and there's that typical drop when you're on a roller coaster ride and the car is falling straight down and I have lost complete control of my car. The car flies off the expressway and I'm believing in my mind that I will die.*

LA, female

Response

Going down the roller coaster road means the way you are achieving your goal in life is harming your mind and body. This is a health dream that bears responding to. Step back for a moment and take an inventory: how many hours sleep do you get a night? Are they restful? Are you tired or energized during the day? Grumpy or engaging? How's your diet? Exercise for mind and body? Do you have meaningful and fulfilling relationships with others? Do you feel you are contributing to something greater than yourself? These questions may help you identify the area(s) that could undergo renovations so that road straightens out a bit and you can maintain control of your car in that dream.

Years ago I had a recurring dream that reminded me of a cover of a Yes album from the early '70's. The roads were thin and high in the air, stretching through thin mountain peaks. I'd be traveling on one when suddenly the road ended in mid-air. Once I realized the dream was talking about my tendency to stop in the middle rather than seeing things through to completion I changed my attitude and the dream stopped. That message was no longer needed to help me grow. My consciousness had changed.

191

DREAM IMAGE

I read the article in the April 30 Springfield News and
Leader about the dream hotline. From Feb. to June
1998. I was in two different hospitals with Three
health problems that could be fatal by themselves. I
had all three at the same time. During Feb. and early
March I had a recurring dream or vision similar to the
image on the enclosed attachment. I would like to
know what you can tell me about this.
JLM, male

Response

John,

This image looks like a bird to us. A bird represents
compulsive ways of thinking in your subconscious
mind. This may be some understanding or ability you
have such as honesty, courage, peace, generosity, or
patience. It is important to draw out and give your
understandings to others.

If you can give us any more information about the
dream we will be able to help you further with it. (The
bird you draw does look like the American Eagle, a
symbol often identified with the United States.)

In regards to the health problems you experienced
we can help you as well. We have found you can heal
your Self of any disorder or disease through visualization, and transforming your daily thoughts and attitudes.
If you would like us to send you more information on
this we can send you information about our healing
projections, intuitive health analyses, or our books on
healing. Please let us know how can aid you.

MANDRAKE ROOT

I had the most unusual symbol in a dream last night: a mandrake root.

That was all that was in the dream. Any comments?
LL, female, Los Angeles, CA

Response

Throughout history the root of mandrake has been used to promote conception, as a cathartic, or as a narcotic and soporific. You were not eating it so it would not indicate any of these, just the *potential* for them in your subconscious existence. In symbolic form that would be creating new ideas, banishing old ones, or denying their existence altogether.

FALLING *in a dream...*

When I was a little girl I had a recurring dream..

You all know the story of the Old Woman Who Lived In A Shoe right? Well, I remember the very first dream I ever had in this series of dreams that went on for at least 3 years. The very first time I had the dream I saw this huge old boot. I knew it was from the Old Lady Who Lived In a Shoe, so I climbed up the ladder to the top. Once at the top I looked in and saw absolutely nothing except pitch black. I decided to climb in anyway. When I went inside it was so dark I couldn't see anything. Suddenly I was falling and thump I landed on a platform. I was relieved that I had stopped falling, and laid on the platform. All of the sudden I was falling off the platform. I hadn't done anything, and I hadn't felt anything push me, but nonetheless I was falling. Soon I landed on another platform and was relieved to be there. This time I tried to stay on the platform, but again, soon I was falling. The dream would just go on like that, and all the subsequent dreams that I had of it would just start with me on a platform and then falling off, all the while being completely black inside.

KL, female, Logan, UT

Response

Although the symbols may be unique in this childhood dream, the message is quite common. The soul, newly clothed in a physical body (symbolized by the boot), must adjust to its new world of experience. The lack of awareness (blackness) while in the inner levels of consciousness is common during the dreamstate. Just as the child is slowly learning how to physically communicate his/her needs and desires through the use of words and gestures, so the child must learn to mentally communicate within self and with others. As a race, we are much better at the first than the second.

The process of falling onto platforms documents the dreamer's attention moving outward toward the physical body and waking state. It is the detailed process of moving from one level of awareness to the next which is why it keeps occurring. The lack of understanding of what is happening is represented by the black inside.

Children are open to subconscious mind. They move freely in and out of the levels of consciousness until they learn how to close-off the inner minds. Teaching children the meaning of dreams helps them value life. It keeps the doorway open between conscious mind and subconscious mind, giving the child the power to become a more self aware adult later in life.

Childhood Nightmare

When I was a little girl I had a recurring dream (it happened about twice a year or so). It was actually a nightmare.

There were huge rocks all around me that gave me a funny feeling in my hands when I looked at them, almost like it would feel really gross to touch them. Next I would see little tiny perfume bottles and delicate glasses, so tiny that they would almost be too small for a Barbie doll to use. I felt like I had to be very careful because the slightest pressure might break them (not to mention that I was surrounded by those nasty rocks and I was afraid they would break them too).

Then I would be walking through this huge forest of very very tall pine trees. Just walking along, and all of the sudden they would start falling all around me. Crash, Crash. It kept getting faster and faster and they were falling all around me. I ran as fast as I could, but I could never seem to get away from them (I never was hit by one though). So I would be running and running with them falling all around me. The next thing I knew I would wake up standing next to my parents' bed wringing my hands trying to get rid of the icky feeling from the rock and holding all of those small things

K*, female

Response

Another childhood dream that reflects the soul's attempts to adjust to the new world. Here the child's stubbornness (*symbolized by the huge rocks*) is affecting her purpose (*hands*). She sees what she receives as inadequate and this is tied to her stubbornness. Here refuge is subconscious existence, the world of dreams and "imaginary" playmates and the like. But this too is becoming overwhelming. She neither belongs in the soul's world or in the material world. She is running and running.

We call this stage growing up. Savvy adults laughingly call it the "terrible 2's" implying that the second year is when every child goes through the "No!" phase. However, this is not true. Some two-year-olds are never taught "No!" so they don't mimic it. It is possible to acknowledge will power – the combination of intelligence and will – from even before birth. Such awareness on the part of the parents helps the soul's transition into the physical plane.

The child knows the pain of experiences left ignored or misunderstood. Have you ever told your child, "It was just a dream" or "It wasn't real". Your child knows better. We must learn to parent the soul of our children as well as the body. Learning how to work with your own dreams is a first step toward that ideal.

High School FOOTBALL

hi,
i am a 45 year old male, and i have had a recurring
dream for years.

*it is that i am getting dressed to go to play in one of
my high school football games, i am usually getting
dressed at home (for some reason?) but often it is in
the locker room of my school. when i get dressed at
home, my mom is driving me to the game and she
either never makes it there, or we forget some part
of my uniform and have to return home to get it and
i am late for or miss the game. if it is in the locker
room, there is always a part of my equipment or
uniform missing and i try to either get in touch with
someone at home (mom) to bring it to me or i try to
go get it myself and again i never make it back or
get it there in time for the game.*

i feel such a tremendous sense of disappointment when i
awaken after these dreams , and they occur frequently, i
would say at least 3 times a month. please let me know
the meaning of this, so i can try to come to terms with it.
Thanks
RH, male

Response

This dream is talking about your approach to life, how you see yourself in relationship to the people and events occurring in your life. You are motivated by competition. The dream tells you your greatest fulfillment however will come from elevating your motivations. This is reflected in the presence of your mom representing your divinity, your inner authority. In both scenarios there is something missing in your outer expression represented by the problems with clothes or equipment. You don't have what it takes so you miss the game. The dream is quite positive because it lets you know there is a higher calling to your life than you now realize, a greater motivating passion that you have yet to become aware of.

Suggestions....Identify what you feel you lack in experience. What skills would add to your confidence? Is it gaining more information? Then take a course, read books, or associate with those who know what you want to know. Is it communication you need? Then learn to think in pictures, practice aligning your mental pictures with words that describe them, and talk anywhere, anytime, with anyone. These are places to start.

As for your purpose in life....Prayer and meditation are essential for connection with your superconscious mind. One of the **FULL SPECTRUM** weekends at the College of Metaphysics is designed to introduce you to both. You might want to check it out at www.som.org

DREAM WORDS

I have some understanding of this and have done quite well interpreting but have one of my own that I can't possibly interpret.....

"Until you make peace with who you are, you'll never be content with what you have" -

MM, female

Response

This dream is short on interpretative symbols. Questions to ask: who said it? A male or female? Someone known or not known? It is a bit of wisdom to contemplate, and could have come from telepathic communication from a guide or teacher. Mind to mind communication happens every day, we just need to become aware of it.

Dreaming Constantly

I hope that you might be able to help me out. I've been having trouble falling asleep at night for some reason. When I am asleep though it seems that I dream constantly. When I awaken I still feel tired and I do not feel refreshed at all. I try to keep in touch with my dreams and discern their meaning, and recently have done it more. I bought the book **The Dreamer's Dictionary**, and it has helped a great deal. I was wondering if I am becoming in touch with my subconscious so much that it is affecting my conscious mind when I wake up. I would appreciate any helpful advice that you could give.

Thank You
BB, male, KY

Response

Trouble falling asleep occurs when we have trouble letting go of the day's experiences. Remedies are completing projects and reviewing the day's accomplishments can relax the mind, bringing a sense of reward and fulfillment making rest easier. Dreaming constantly indicates your attention is still in the physical world. When you wrestle with yourself all night you wake up tired. Relax before retiring. Meditate. Take a warm bath or shower. Get a massage. Exercise for half an hour. Whatever works for you. You can also communicate your desire to your subconscious mind by writing and reading a message that communicates your need for deeper sleep.

What you describe is not so much your subconscious affecting your conscious mind as it is overworking your conscious mind. Let go, so your subconscious mind can perform its function of rejuvenation.

READING *in your dreams*

I used to hate it when I was dreaming of reading.
The words would swirl and change while you
read. If I read the same thing twice it would be
different. I made a supreme effort to read anything in a dream and I got better and better at it
until the text started to make sense.

That was until my subconscious mind put
me in place.

I was dreaming that I was reading a scientific
manual and as the text became clearer I realized
that what I was reading was something that was
almost like the 'Answer of Life'. I tried harder
and harder to read until some letters swirled
around and formed the only readable bit of text
that said, 'Don't be a smart ass, show off!'.

I was startled awake with the shock, and no
matter how I tried, I couldn't remember what had
been written in the text. All I remember is that
the concept is so simple, so obvious, that we have
been looking at all the time and not realizing it.

Do you think that maybe we all do have the
answers to life and the meta-physical world but
are too programmed by sociological programming that we can't access the information?

D*, male, Hobart Tasmania, Australia.

Response

The progression of your dream does indicate a great way to get your attention. When books and writings appear in dreams they symbolize the dreamer's need for information. Dreams of this nature often indicate an over-saturation of brain stimulation, a reliance upon intellect in place of bringing out all parts of self.

Programming is not bad, a certain amount is needed for mental and physical efficiency. What we need is education for the whole Self. For thousands of years that type of education has been in monasteries around the world not openly available. How humanity will change in the times to come as education that nurtures and challenges spiritual, mental, emotional, and physical development becomes commonplace. It is this kind of education the School of Metaphysics is dedicated to providing in order to accelerate the evolution of humanity.

As a footnote, I have read of several accounts where people slept with texts or books in their aura in order to absorb the material. I wasn't so sure about that until I remembered a time when I was a teenager. I fell asleep while reading a mystery novel, when I woke up it was still lying on my stomach. As I finished reading the book it was like I'd already read it, but I knew I hadn't. It would be years before I would hear of these accounts and begin to understand what must have occurred. It's worth experimenting with for the scientifically minded.

'Wake up! *You're Dreaming*'

As a child I had a few reoccurring dreams but two of them stand out.

In one dream *I would be returning from a walk in the bush with a friend and when we walked from the bush onto the end of our street I would be in front of my friend, I would turn to him and say the same thing each time I had the dream (I can't remember what it was). As I turned back I would have to walk through a large white steel vehicle barrier at the end of the street. In real life this barrier was not there. I would always frown at the barrier and wonder why it was there.*

I would have this dream about once a month for 2-3 years then I had it less and less until it stopped. Many years later the council built the gate but I had forgotten the dream by then until a couple of months later we were walking through the gate just like in the dream. I turned and said something to my friend, turned back and frowned at the gate, and said 'wake up stupid, your dreaming'. My head shot up as I realized that this time it was real. I turned to my friend, and I kid you not, at the same time we pointed at each other and said 'It finally happened!'.

It turns out that my friend also had been having this dream but in his dream I kept saying 'wake up stupid, you're dreaming' instead of just walking on. What do you make of that? BH, Australia

Response

Your dream symbolized a well known aspect of yourself that you relied upon to reach your goal but you would give in when you met up with an obstacle. Your friend's dream indicates he went on to achieve his goal. The goals may have been and probably were different.

When the physical event occurred it stimulated the memory placed in your brain as a child. The fact that both of you had such similar dreams reflects your connectedness. Shared dreams are a reality. They are inner level experiences in subconscious mind occurring when people are on the same wavelength. Just as we enjoy our friends in our waking life, so we can learn to become aware of enjoying them in subconscious mind.

This is the future of human consciousness. Because the dreams differ, there is not strong evidence that you and your friend shared the dream experience but it does indicate you had a great deal in common in your states of awareness at the time of the dreams.

Return of the
GRIM REAPER

I frequently had this nightmare where
*I had to take something down across the road
from my parent's house to a neighbor's at night.
As I would cross the road I would look to the
right and see that there was a thick fog about 10
meters (33 feet) away with a couple of street
lights making it glow. I would see these dark
areas in the fog that looked like tall cloaked
figures, a bit like the Grim Reaper. I would freeze
to the spot and try to scream but nothing would
come out.*

*At this time another family member would
wake me up saying that I was thrashing around
on the bed and moaning. Well, one night I had to
take a miss-addressed letter across to the same
house and, as you can guess, there was the back
lit fog, and the dark shapes. I froze for a moment,
then somehow turned and faced them and
screamed at the top of my voice. I then ran across
the road and posted the letter. As I ran back home
I looked towards the shapes and they, and the fog,
were gone, like they had never been there.*

Have fun analyzing these and I hope that they are
entertaining.
DN, male.

Response

As we have talked about before there are commonalities in childhood dreams. You had a goal in life but it was unclear how you would accomplish it. In your search to know how you met with unknown aspects of self that scared you.

The element of wanting to scream and not being able to is also common for children. This is because the dream was a nightmare where you were not in control. You did not understand the energies. You were experiencing something new in your environment and you didn't know how to express that experience.

When your dream "came true" you took control in your waking state and found the fog and grim reapers had disappeared.

NIGHT TERRORS

My daughter is six years old. Since she was about two or three she has been experiencing horrible nightmares. There were times, especially when she was younger, that they would occur every night about the same time and sometimes continue for several hours. As she has gotten older they seem to happen less frequently. She wakes up screaming and when I come into the room she does not know that I am there. She seems to be awake, but does not easily respond to my questions and seems to see things around her. She shakes and is obviously terrified. She sometimes repeats the same word or phrase over and over.

As you can imagine this is extremely frightening for me as a mother. However, she does not remember the dream. The only thing that we have found that helps is to get her out of bed and into another room that is well lit. Then we get her some water and talk to her. Sometimes we get her to say her ABC's or sing a song. Anything that would get her to wake up a little.

The only thing that I have found that seems close to what she experiences is night terrors. I do not know that much about them, but I would like to know if you believe this is what is happening and why it is happening. I also would like to know what I can do to help her. I would appreciate any help that you can give me. Or if you know someone that specializes in this sort of thing please let me know. I heard a man from this school on 107.5 WKZL in Greensboro, NC and wondered if you may be able to help me. Thank you for your time.

TS, mother

Response

Your response is quite natural. Why getting your daughter out of bed, into the light, drinking and singing works is because it brings all of her attention back into the physical and away from whatever was happening that she couldn't interpret or understand. Being a parent I can imagine how disconcerting and truly frightening this can be to a parent who loves their child.

Our child is now five and it is only recently that he has been willing to give himself to sleep. For the first 3 and a half years he was restless throughout the night, waking or making sounds and later talking frequently. He would sit up in bed, eyes wide open and talk to you, but still be in subconscious mind. My husband's and my experience with dreamstates were a real boon to understanding Hezekiah's state of consciousness and those alleviating any fear. In the first two years I would mentally take him by the hand and literally lead him into the dreamstate. Intuitive Health Analyses also gave excellent recommendations for helping him.

Suggestions.....realize crying is normal in a child who has yet to learn how to communicate his/her thoughts about experience. Whether awake or asleep, crying is the natural means to get attention. Encourage your child to talk about his experience. Then seek to understand it. Childrens' dreams will tell you the state of their awareness and that information is invaluable to every parent. Also take care in the books your child reads, the television or movies he sees. Not just before going to bed but throughout the day. Images get into children's minds and remain there. Make sure your child is exposed to the world you want him or her to know. One based on your highest ideals and expectations not your fears.

The *VOLCANO* and *YACHT*

I had this dream just a few days ago and it has sort of been bugging me..

In my dream, there was a national disaster about to happen and it was all over the news. The news was reporting that a huge volcano was about to erupt and when it did, it would take out most of the United States, only leaving the east coast. I was very upset in the dream because they were saying that the hot lava would cover the mountains and middle part of the state of North Carolina too(where we live). The only part of our state that would remain would be from Raleigh to the coast.

At the same time of this national disaster, my fiance and I found out that our friends, Stacy and Brian, had just finalized everything to rent a yacht to live on. Since our friends wanted us to see their new home, they invited us over for dinner and drinks before this volcano erupted.

Before going to their new home, I went to consult with my best friend's mom, who I have known since kindergarten. Now, she has always been able to sort of see things, and predict things pretty well. The weird thing is she lives in Nor-folk, VA, where I met her daughter (my best friend) and grew up myself. So in the dream I am asking her, will we be hurt by this volcano and such. Well, she tells me that she sees that Brian will be killed and that Stacy is pregnant and does not know yet.

So then all of a sudden in the dream, it jumps from being with my best friend's mom to my fiance and I on our way to their yacht. Stacy and Brian are leading us to their new place, but you have to go through this tiny shack that is full of people, up a narrow flight of stairs, and down a long hallway just to get on the yacht. I remem-ber feeling so emotional because even though I had told my fiance about what I learned from my best friend's mom, I could not decide whether to tell Stacy and Brian. I remember feeling so bad, especially if all that I was told came true-Brian dying, Stacy being pregnant.

Then I woke up--never knew if the disaster happened or not. What does all this mean??
GG, female

Response

The dreamer is experiencing an openness and expansiveness in her life that she thinks is beyond her control. She expects a great deal of change to come from it that again she does not want but what can she do? She believes it will change everything that is familiar to her, particularly certain patterns of thinking symbolized by she and her fiance and Stacy and Brian, a conscious and subconscious aspect of herself. She is attempting to bring knowledge into herself and a temporary mindset.

Insight from a superconscious aspect reveals that the subconscious aspect symbolized by Brian is going to change and the conscious aspect symbolized by Stacy is going to produce a new way of life. In order for this to happen aspects must come out of subconscious mind into the physical, everyday life and be expressed. This is affecting the dreamer's emotions causing indecision about what she will think or do.

Suggestions....embrace the change. Stop fighting it. Become decisive by imaging your ideal of a new and better way of life. A new and better you. This will guide the impending change and you will no longer be a victim.

HUSBAND

Greetings SOM:
I keep dreaming of my husband. I know he
represents an aspect committed to wholeness.
Sometimes we are in a house (mind) and sometimes outside. What does it mean when he is
outside with me?

Are there dreams that represent other people in
your life and their role? Is everyone all the time
representing an aspect?

MM, female, St. Louis

Response

When you are outside with your spouse in a dream it is
indicating how you are using both conscious and subconscious minds. The action will describe the use. For
instance if you and your husband are at a football game
the dream is telling you about how you approach life. If
the two of you are at a restaurant eating, the dream is
talking about knowledge you are receiving that adds to
your conscious and your subconscious minds.

Even in prophetic and clairvoyant dreams, people
represent aspects of yourself. There are such things as
inner level experiences, just as there are experiences in
the physical world. These are unique for movement is
determined by thought.

LOST

I was in a car with 2 other girls. We were lost, driving through a thick, very dark forest. The road was very windy and we couldn't see what was ahead because it was so dark. We kept driving and as we did, cars would appear just before another turn

I have no idea what this could mean......if you do, great. It has been several months since I had this dream. But I still remember it like it really happened, every little detail. I have thought about it a lot....and have come to no conclusions.

JW, female

Response

There are specific symbols in your dream. The car represents your physical body, the girls known conscious aspects. You, with these aspects, are in control of your life. The dream is pointing out you need to set a goal. Without it you are mentally, spiritually, and emotionally "lost". Even when you are aware that you do not have a direction you insist upon persisting.

This is the meat of the dream – at the time you had the dream you were directionless yet kept going, expending energy. At the time, you needed to stop, look at your life honestly, see your opportunities and choose those you truly desire. This would bring "light" into your life as well as a direction.

You can still do this now. When you've done so the dream will no longer haunt you.

WHY do recurring dreams happen?

greetings!! i am making a study about recurring dreams and I need your help by answering a few questions. I would want to find out why recurring dreams happen and what are the messages or hidden meaning it wishes to convey to the dreamer. I hope you can send me more information about recurring dreams aside from the questions I asked. I would really appreciate your help. Thank you very much and hoping for your kind consideration!

ACO, female

Response
Recurring dreams happen because the dreamer's state of awareness is the same, it has not changed. It's like sending someone the same letter or e-mail until they acknowledge receiving it and respond. Recurring dreams are the subconscious mind sending the same message until it is received by the conscious mind and a response is formed.

The messages are as varied as people, but a study of recurring dreams could be quite revealing for the individual as well as windows into collective attitudes.

A DARK SPIRIT VISITS AT 3 AM

I had a dream where I was sleeping and dreaming. I was awakened by a spirit entering the room. I could see its chakras and its body shape then his head revealed the face of someone who has been on TV (a man) and became famous. Though this face looked more feminine as it had eyeliner on the eyes. It spoke to me through telepathy and said someone would contact me soon. I felt that the spirit was a dark spirit with evil intentions as everything around me felt dark and scary and that it wanted someone to abuse me sexually. I told it to leave and it did.

Then there was a knock at the door. so I asked who it was and it replied that it wanted to talk with me. Because i felt i had met an evil spirit and it was supposed to be 3 am in the morning I told the person to go away and it did.

Then I totally awoke from the dream and saw an energy right next to the drawing of my ex-girlfriend who i have quarreled with. Then I heard a knock at the door and presumed it must have been the energy or a spirit. I opened my window took deep breaths, recited the lords prayer and went back to sleep. The funny thing was it was also 3 am.

SAH, female

Response

Because we are experiencing in subconscious mind during sleep, we can have a variety of experiences. At first, they will all tend to appear to us as dreams. This is because humanity is only now beginning to develop human consciousness into spiritual consciousness. This dream can be interpreted in symbolic form but the way you describe the action indicates this was an inner level experience. You actually were perceiving in subconscious mind an entity separate from yourself. The most important truth to keep in mind is that because you exist in the physical plane you are more powerful than any entity that exists only in the inner levels. That is why when you told him to leave he did. Remember this. There are many historical accounts of visitations during the dream state. Your action of filling your mind with harmony and truth was a wise one, for the Law of Attraction is a reality in all worlds.

High School Sweetheart

Salutations,
I am new to your site, having just recently heard about it on the radio. For the first time since then, I have had a dream I remember, and one that rather mystified me, so I decided to give this a try.

As the dream begins, *I am in a rather well-to-do home (more impressive than my current one to be sure) with my two daughters (who do not exist in real life). In the dream, my wife has since passed away (also, not true in reality, we have just celebrated our 3 year anniversary). It seems that I have named one of my daughters Sarah (my high school sweetheart, who remains a good friend to this day.), on an impulse, I give her a call, asking if she might visit. She replies that she hasn't the money, to which I say isn't a problem, I will pay for her ticket. The ticket cost tallies up to over 3,000 dollars (a bit odd, no?), to which I cringe at, as if I may not have money to cover, but resolve to deal with it anyhow. The remainder of the dream is fairly sketchy to me, but it seems that Sarah and I court for a week or two, and just before I wake up, I get an image of her courting another man behind my back. The man is unrecognizable (to me), but in the dream is a trusted associate.*

Well, there it is, I hope you can make something out of it, and I thank you for your time.
JP, male

Response

This dream is telling you the state of your awareness which is why it is different from your physical life situation. You see a great deal of worth in your mind including your subconscious mind symbolized by the daughters. In order to create what you want in your life you need to value the aspect of yourself symbolized by Sarah, the old sweetheart. You are willing to do so but for some reason feel betrayed by this part of yourself. The key does not lie in Sarah but in the unknown man – he is a conscious aspect you are not aware of and you fear that aspect will get what it wants rather than you getting what you want. Keep in mind the man is you. You are always in control. Determine what Sarah represents to you (what is her strongest quality in your eyes?) and begin consciously harmonizing with that aspect, using it in your thinking about yourself and your life.

ANTICHRIST

i need help. i have had a couple of dreams that i really need interpreted.

the first was me walking down the street and noticing panic in everyone. someone told me the sun was supposed to burn out and god was coming back. i laughed.

then...walking down same street....same people...and sun burns out. suddenly i doubt everything in life. i run to find loved ones. i see president on TV praying for everyone. He tells us to go to our church for a tv broadcast from a man who is supposed to let us know what to do next. i struggle hard to get loved ones in the church. husband wouldn't go. after in church with all loved ones....doors slam close...and the man is actually in my church...he raises his hand and smiles and in that moment, i realize i have led my loved ones to evil....i don't know if he was the anti-christ or what...but i just knew it was wrong...

i woke up and thought it was all real....most realistic dream ever....this is a brief summary of it...but i literally remember EVERY detail....then about 5 months later i had another one similar....but in the end... it ended better..with a man wiping my tears and telling me everything would be taken care of...and then he vanished....help
JIC, female

Response

Your dream indicates a change in the way you understand your divinity, your inner authority. It has affected all parts of you. Existing ideas of spirituality are no longer serving you and you know they will not lead you where you desire to go. So does your subconscious mind, symbolized by your husband (he's the one who doesn't go to the church). You have a better idea of what will bring wholeness and healing than those you've settled for in the past.

The second version of the dream indicates you have turned this dilemma over to your subconscious mind thus feeling more at peace. In the process known as visualization there comes a time when the conscious mind releases the object of its desire to the subconscious mind for reproduction. This is what you have done.

SLOW MOTION

I have a recurring thing that happens when I dream.

I often dream that someone is trying to do me bodily harm, and I have a gun. When I shoot at the person(s), the bullets fly slowly through the air (slow slowly I watch them fly across the room), and hit the person like a rubber eraser would if thrown at them.

To get away, I usually have the ability to fly, but just high enough that I am out of reach. The Person can usually reach me if they jump or reach out, but I usually just slip away as they grab for me.

I probably have a dream like this once or twice per month.

I also often dream that the US is under attack (war) with another country, and I am usually in a house of some sort, and trying to find a secure place to hide where I cannot be found. I usually search for all kinds of areas, mostly looking for a place to get in the attack areas of the house, but never seem to find the "right" place.

MT, female

Response

There are three distinct symbols here: the slow motion bullets, flying, and the war.

First, slow motion. When we sleep energy is removed from our outer consciousness and directed inward for revitalization and communication. There are four distinct expressions of consciousness (we call them levels) in the subconscious mind where dreaming occurs. Slow motion dreams occur because the attention is divided between the conscious and subconscious minds. It's like you haven't caught up with yourself so you appear to move in slow motion. Once the conscious attention is aligned with the subconscious attention the action will begin to move as you are used to, in "real" time. Your "Matrix"- like dream is a common one. Learning how to harness the power of your attention is so vitally important to self awareness and the development of consciousness that it is the first skill we teach.

Second, flying. The act of lifting off the ground and flying in a dream is also a common symbol representing the dreamer's capacity to move in the inner levels of subconscious mind. This is described as astral projecting or an out-of-body experience and happens every night when we sleep. All attention is removed from the physical body and our inner attention is free to explore these immaterial worlds often revealed to us during "dream states". Flying dreams often indicate how we are responding to freedom in our lives. Since someone is trying to grab you during your dream flight this dream is pointing out that unknown parts of yourself are attempting to hold you down. If they are male, you need to start seeing your inner self as a friend rather than a foe. If they are female, start looking for ways you sabotage yourself by trying to do everything yourself.

Third, the war. **The Dreamer's Dictionary** states,

"War is a violent contest fought for many purposes from territorial to religious but always with an economical undercurrent. In the Universal Language of Mind it symbolizes inner conflict that is destructive to the dreamer. Conflict is destructive to the thinker because the lack of resolve drains the will, disperses the attention, and scatters mental energy away from positive, productive ends. Individual conflict embodies the opposing viewpoint of good and evil."

In your dream you try to hide from the conflict and are never quite able to accomplish your goal. This is actually to your credit, for it will be easier for you to face your turmoil and resolve it. Look at your life. How do you determine what is right? Does your sense of right guide your thoughts and actions or is it merely a means to pass judgement on others while you remain undisciplined? Resolve inner conflicts by employing your power of reasoning. Envision the outcome of your present thinking and action. Choose that which will bring peace and understanding to your Self and others.

Do you meditate? If not, you might consider beginning as a means to build upon the abilities your dreams reflect.•

You can become an interpreter of dreams!

Learning to interpret your dreams is like learning a new language. You have a means to communicate your thoughts to others that was previously out of your reach. Everyone dreams, just as most everyone speaks and hears. To wield language, we learn how to read and write. To understand the meaning in dream communications, we learn mental skills of concentration, recall, and reasoning. These then become the foundation for lucid dreaming and eventually transcendent awareness. This book introduces you to the basics of dreaming.

We share much of our research into humanity's potential through the Internet. Our virtual campus at www.som.org has a sister campus devoted entirely to dream study. Here you will find transcripts of interviews, lessons, and chats with the foremost authorities in this field. You can receive lessons for study in your own home. By visiting www.dreamschool.org, you have thousands of questions answered, hundreds of dream symbols at your fingertips and dozens of dreams interpreted.

The best way to learn is to study at a School of Metaphysics where you will have a teacher and fellow students to learn with. There are sixteen schools throughout the greater Midwest (US).

If you live elsewhere in the States or world, we offer a correspondence study program with a graduate student here at the College of Metaphysics. You will learn the principles of the laws that govern creation and how to harmonize with them for greater effectiveness, success, happiness, and awareness. Everything you learn at this study is about the most important

225

person in your world – YOU! Dreams are as Freud said, "The royal road to Self awareness."

If you want to set the pace of your learning, don't live near a school, or for some reason are not ready for weekly study, use this site to embark on an independent, self study program. Investigate "How to Use this Site" for suggestions. There are hundreds of dreams with commentary available here, and the research continues so new information is constantly made available. Many have used what they learn here for papers and course credit through colleges and universities.

Online Mentor Program

Sometimes it helps to have a mentor, a counselor, to understand the meaning of your dreams. The **Dream of the Month Club** has been created to fulfill this need. The **Dream of the Month Club** is an online mentor program for you to receive personal instruction each month. Members receive timely information and study materials for deepening their understanding of dreams each week by email.

Each month you can email to us a dream for interpretation. A psi counselor skilled in the art and science of dream interpretation will give you an in-depth interpretation of a dream similar to those found in case histories appearing on the next few pages and in the "How to Interpret Your Dreams" and "Common Themes" sections www.dreamschool.org website. Your dream (and questions) will be responded to near the end of the month.

The first week of each month a detailed case history of a someone's dream is emailed to you. This dream will include the breakdown of the meaning of symbols and the interpretation of the dream. The description of how the dream fits into the dreamer's life will help you understand how to interpret your own dreams and relate them to what's going on during your waking hours.

The next week "dreamschool Focus" teaches you easily and quickly about how to get the most from your dream time. It keeps remembering your dreams in your consciousness so your subconscious mind can work on your behalf. The focus may be on what your dreams say about your health, the causes for sleepwalking/talking/eating/etc., harnessing dreams for problem solving and success, or how to break patterns of thought that prompt nightmares.

Near the end of the month you receive an article concerning an in-depth exploration of a Creative Mind analysis. The Creative Mind analysis is a kind of Intuitive Report developed by the School of Metaphysics which gives an amazing account of how a person is using his waking mind and his inner, subconscious dreaming mind. These reports elucidate truths that apply to all of us. The articles are written by the person (or someone who interviewed them) who received the report and include their insights and discoveries. They are an education in how to use our full potential as creative beings.

The best part about being a member of the Dream of the Month Club is having a mentor. Being a club member ensures that you receive answers when you need them. It connects you with others who are serious about using their dreams fully, and affords you a consistent and convenient way to build an invaluable skill. Joining the Dream of the Month Club is easy. Visit http://www.dreamschool.org to sign up or email us at club@dreamschool.org to receive membership information.

The Creative Mind Analysis
The last week of each month Dream of the Month Club Members participate in our ongoing intuitive research. The School of Metaphysics has been invested in this type of research since its forming in the late 1960's. Decades later, an entire section of

the school's website is devoted to the incredible amount of data collected on the relationship between mind and body (Intuitive Health Analyses), the continuity of existence and the reality of the soul (Past Life Profiles), and relationships between souls (Past Life Crossings and Family Profiles). Over 100,000 intuitive reports have been done for people on six continents, all members of the Society for Intuitive Research (SIR).

Perhaps the most amazing part of this research, and certainly the part that attests to its longevity and the need for it in the future, is its science. The information – even if it dates from Atlantis and other previously unrecorded times – is always relevant to the individual and his or her life now. This is significant research opening the doors to what lies beyond human potential. Through intuitive research people can learn what their purpose is, how to help their child, when to make a business move, why situations repeat themselves in their lives, and who they were in a past life or who they can become in the present one.

Since the mid-1990's my husband Daniel Condron and I have taken intuitive research into new directions, exploring the reality of spiritual man in today's world. Our dedication to this work has endowed us with exceptional ability to probe the inner levels of consciousness on other's behalf. What is surfacing in this research is truly changing the way we understand ourselves and our world.

For instance, the Atlantean Profiles are not so much rewriting history on this planet as extending the written record far beyond the 8000 years commonly found in cultures around the world. Some of this research is catalogued in **Remembering Atlantis: The History of the World Vol. 1**. The Dharma profiles answer the question "Why am I here?" by revealing the soul's duty, the inner Self's purpose for life on earth. This intuitive report gives focus to the one receiving the information. The clarity of the description of how the dharma came about resonates with each person often enabling them to release fears and understand the reason for the people, places, and situations throughout his/her life.

The Transference of Energy reports examine how the individual uses Infinite Energy. It reads like a futuristic health report, analyzing the flow of energy through the chakra system. Which chakras are being drawn upon and which are neglected is described in detail along with the insight to make adjustments that will lead to greater self control, fulfillment and enlightenment.

These and four additional types of intuitive reporting are offered only in person during Spiritual Focus Sessions held throughout the year on the College of Metaphysics campus. More information on these can be gained at www.som.org

During the session called "Genius!" a Creative Mind report is given. This intuitive report elucidates the individual's ability and skill in visualizing. It details how they are using the conscious mind and subconscious mind to create and fulfill their desires. This is the report we share with you as a Dream of the Month Club member because it will give you valuable insight into your own potential as a creator while deepening your understanding of the importance of your dreams. Night time dreams are the subconscious mind's opportunity to "speak its mind", to offer feedback to the conscious mind. Your daytime dreams are the way the conscious mind tells the subconscious mind what it desires. Since the subconscious mind's duty is to fulfill the conscious mind's desires, the quality of your thinking becomes important. The more aware you are, the more informed you can be.

An Experience With A Creative Mind Report
by Jonathan Duerbeck

I first heard a creative mind report in October, 2002 during my class in Mastery of Consciousness in the School of Metaphysics. This report is presented to SOM students in the third cycle of lessons, as well as participants in a weekend experience called a Spiritual Focus Weekend. The School of Metaphysics teaches people to be mental creators, and the Creative Mind Report describes how a person uses their conscious and subconscious divisions of mind to create. My classmates and I were at the College of Metaphysics to hear our reports in person. I heard a description of how each my classmates were using their creative mind. My report was last and I was nervous.

"This one tends to be self-consumed. We see that this one resides in the brain and therefore there is the attempt to associate, to create, to connect, to cause mental motion through brain patterns. This is highly frustrating for this one, and yet we see that this one has not caused there to be a different way of responding to the outer or inner world than this same pattern. Therefore, this one keeps getting the same result. We see that it is the repetition of this that is a signal for this one that something that this one is doing is not working. However, we see that this one continues to ignore it." (10-15-02-BGC-7)

I had been told repeatedly that I need to get out of my brain and into my mind, that I need to think mentally instead of physically. I thought I had made some progress in this area. I felt like all the progress I thought I had made had evaporated like a big self-delusion. I felt like I had nothing to show for several years of trying to learn metaphysics. I kept thinking, "OK, OK, I'm sorry, I don't want to be that way, but what do I need to DO?!"

230

I didn't want to be a self-consumed person and I didn't want to be a person who ignores things. That was in the total opposite direction of my ideals and I was finding out that I was exactly what I didn't want to be.

I knew I was often frustrated, especially with myself, and that everything seemed hard and slow. I often felt like I was banging my head into the same limiting situations over and over and didn't see the way out. I would get so frustrated I would punch things and hurt my hand. The report went on to describe why I had such a hard time trying to create anything and how I cut myself off from using my whole mind.

"We see that there is a very real need for this one to become conscious of the fact that this one remains in the thinking processes and does move in rapid fashion ideas that have no substance, that have no bearing or relevance to the inner mind. Therefore, these ideas tend to be barren, and we see that when there is an idea or seed that this one wants to plant and feels strongly about, the inroads to do so are nonexistent. We see that then this one tends to try to understand this through logic, through the brain, rather than through reasoning, which would include the developed and purposeful use of imagination. We see that there are times when this one will image something, where this one will visualize, and we see that ideas are transmitted to subconscious mind. We see they can even undergo a development and expansion. However, we see that when this one gets to the point of discrimination with it, of ... solidifying it, there has, by this point, been a loss of the original seed. The ability for this one to manifest expansion is negligent, and we see that it causes difficulty in this one being able to have what he desires. It causes difficulty in this one being able to create something and manifest it." (10-15-02-BGC-7)

I had often felt like there was something wrong with me, like I was a very slow student in metaphysics and couldn't seem to visualize and manifest things or have the kinds of non-physical experiences other people talked about. Everything seemed very hard and I continually felt overwhelmed, tired, and way behind on everything. I often fluctuated between gratitude and frustration because I have so much to be grateful for, and so much I have not accomplished. The subconscious or inner mind was like some kind of magic faraway thing that I would someday experience, like Heaven. Something was indeed wrong and I truly was not using my subconscious mind whatsoever. Then I got the answer of what to do about it.

"We see that there is a need for this one to recognize that this" *(inability to create with the inner mind)* *"is a reflection of the promulgation of ideas and thoughts in the brain that have no direct bearing or relationship to the soul. It is the changing of this that will enable this one to have more self-possession in a true sense. We see that often this one's present form of self-possession is limitation that then leads to separation from others, to argumentation, to rejection of others. Would suggest that this one begin to define the self by something other than his ideas, and to base his assessment of self and others upon more permanent virtues or characteristics. This would be an excellent exercise to aid this one in becoming free of the old patterns of thinking that this one so easily falls prey to."* (10-15-02-BGC-7)

I thought I had recognized that I scattered my thinking, since that was something I had been told repeatedly by my teachers. I thought I had taken it for granted that I was scattered, and that stilling the mind was the solution to pretty much anything for me. Again, I cringed and to hear that I was exactly what I didn't

232

want to be - someone who argues and judges and rejects people. I see now what was meant by using limitation to have self-possession. I would feel overwhelmed, and to get a grip on myself, I would say no to things or try to simplify life or save time by eliminating something. I would feel overwhelmed by reactions to people and I avoided whatever I reacted to, thinking I couldn't function otherwise. A couple months after this report, I practiced confronting whatever I had avoided, especially people. There were people I felt a lot of tension with that I talked to directly and stopped avoiding. I had a motto for a while of "peace through conflict." I wanted to have the courage and will to renounce any kind of avoidance and go through anything so I could have peace of mind.

"We see that it would also be important for this one to be attentive to the dreams, for this one needs to learn how to think in pictures. This one has the ability to visualize in the physical conscious mind. However, this one does not understand the relationship between the outer and inner mind, as the essence of visualization, and therefore the intelligence of creativity. As this one is able to slow the mind, so that there can be images placed with each...correction...so that there can be images which the words and actions describe, there will then be the ability to think with the mind rather than the brain. This is all."

I used to think I had a poor imagination, since I wasn't very good at creating things and struggled with visualization exercises. I know now that I actually do have a strong imagination and I can form pictures. So I was confused to hear this. What else did I need to do if I'm visualizing and it's STILL not working? To make the images mental instead of physical means to HOLD them STEADY in mind, believe in them and let them go, as far

233

as I can tell so far.

"Very well. You will also relate that which will foster a movement within the energy exchange between the ethereal and the material for the cultivation of genius."

"This would be in the stilling of the conscious mind, the development of the willpower to be able to keep the attention in the present and upon what is at hand. The development of concentration is essential for this one. The ability to hold the mind steady is important, and we see that this needs to be done with thought as well as with things. We see that there is a need to develop the ability to perceive in pictures, to then describe them with words as has already been given. The development and use of dream states would aid this as well. There is a need for this one to begin to practice the receiving of other people's images. This is very challenging for this one, for we see that this one allows the mind to be busy and in doing so does not allow the impression on his mind substance of images from other people. Therefore, this one remains within his own thinking. Part of this is a defensive, protective device. Part of it is a means by which this one can maintain the distance between the self and others that this one finds more comfortable. This one is still attached to separation, and as long as this idea is ruling the self, there will continue to be separation between the inner and outer self as well. Therefore, in order to utilize more of the mind than is presently being done, this will need to be changed. This is all." (10-15-02-BGC-7)

I became more devoted to spiritual exercises after hearing this report and started doing all of them in the morning whenever possible. I was not at all surprised that I needed to still my mind.

234

That's been the thing I need to do to solve nearly every difficulty I've ever had and I still hadn't accomplished it. I had begun to think of it as an impossible goal that would take me my whole life.

Again, I found out that I was exactly the opposite of my ideals and that didn't feel good. My highest priority for a long time had been to experience connection and I was still attached to separation. That's still my highest priority. I began focusing more on listening to people and letting go of thoughts about what they said or what I could say next. Someone called the school a while later and I focused on totally listening and she told me her life story and cried on the phone and became a student. When one of my students came to our school for the first time, I focused on totally listening and let go of thoughts about things I could teach her based on what she said. She told about how she used to be really depressed and I had tears in my eyes hearing it and that made an impression on her.

"This one says, 'How can I more effectively create with others?'"

"By changing this one's ego. We see that much of this one's identity is caught up in the ideas that this one holds. Therefore there is no room for adjustment, for expansion for others. This one has a natural curiosity that could be the strongest quality within the self to build upon. Would suggest that this one practice becoming just as curious about people and how they think and believe and why and what they do and how they do what they do, as this one is about things and lower life forms."

Here was yet another way I was the opposite of what I wanted to be. So I started letting go of my ideas about how things should be done, especially in directing our school. If someone said, "Let's get rid of this wallpaper," I said "OK" instead of "no, we need to do other things first." I enjoy learning about and experiencing nature (things and lower life forms). So this gave me something I already had that I could expand on. I started asking people more questions and looking at people differently, like observing something I hadn't seen.

"This one says, 'How can I better understand and identify my emotions?'"

"To realize that what this one has learned to identify as emotions is only a limited spread of how they can manifest, that this one has a false belief that he is not emotional, that he is very logical, and very controlled, and very, therefore, right. This is a false belief and a false self-perception. This one is highly emotional in the degree that this one is attached to his ego. And it is in the places where this one begins to separate and to cut off and to blame or judge others that this is most pronounced. It is therefore in the ways in which this one pushes people away." (10-15-02-BGC-7)

I could add "open and accepting" to the list of incorrect self-perceptions. Again, I was not what I thought I was and I was the opposite of what I wanted to be. I didn't want to be egotistical or someone that thinks they're always right and blames and judges and pushes people away. I know I used to like being by myself or away from crowds, and I wasn't very interested in people, but I thought I had made progress on that, too. I know I often wished people would leave so I could relax and then felt guilty about not wanting people around. One thing I did about that was to be willing to feel awkward around people.

236

"This one says, 'How can I be aware of when I am in my brain and when I am in my mind?'"

"When this one is utilizing the mind there is expansion and there is connectedness. They do not have to be caused. They are present."

"How does this one recognize when he is deluding the self into thinking he is thinking in pictures?"

"When this one is nullifying what this one is imaging, this one is staying in the brain and is limited to the body. [This one needs] to break free of negative patterns of thinking. These are stored in the brain. They are not stored in the soul."

For about a month after hearing this report, I felt like I didn't belong in my class, I felt embarrassed to be in the position of directing a school, and I felt I had no business teaching. I felt very ungrounded because I didn't trust my self-perceptions. I felt like I couldn't trust my own self-perceptions since they were so wrong. I wasn't sure how I would know if I changed anything or if I was just deluding myself.

One night I was getting something at Lowes and I thought up a song that helped me accept where I was and move forward. It was a song about being stuck in jail, and deciding that as long as I'm stuck in a jail, I'll be happy and as helpful to other people as I can. I decided that even if I was stuck in my brain and self consumed and all that, I'd be the nicest self-consumed, stuck-in-their brain person I could be. That has helped me to be more relaxed and get some attention off of myself. Then that has led to being more confident, secure, and feeling like I have something to give.

I also remembered something that Dr. Daniel Condron, my class teacher, said. He said, "When all else fails, change." I thought of it as, when you're stuck and don't know what to do, just do something different, anything. So I tried writing my thoughts a lot, choosing to do things I didn't think I had time to do, acting on thoughts I never acted on, whatever. If it was too late to change a repeating physical situation, like being late or cramming last minute things, I allowed myself to have a positive attitude anyway. And I dare to believe I might have had some experiences of a still- or at least stiller -mind.

Intuitive reports are truth. It's true that the truth will set you free. I believe that truth is also beautiful and good, and it only seems ugly or painful when you're in a stuck place that the truth can set you free from. Intuitive reports are for anyone who loves freedom.•

Where to Make Real Spiritual Progress
by Paul Madar

The Intuitive Report I refer to most often is my Creative Mind intuitive report. I received it in the fall of 1997, and ever since then it has become a touchstone for my progress in spiritual growth.

There were particular revelations and suggestions given in that report that I worked to embed in my consciousness. They shaped my choices, beliefs, and perspectives for the years to come, influencing my decisions to become a director, move to the College of Metaphysics for a year of intensive study, and to eventually move to live as staff at the College.

What were these life altering suggestions? The report began by talking about how I love to create, and get a thrill out of creating because so many creative avenues are open to me-

-art, music, writing, carpentry, and so on.

This one has many understandings that are at his command that this one does have the capability of setting into action. We see therefore this one has many different uses for the creative mind in terms of physical expressions of it, and we see that this one derives great enjoyment and a sense of thrill from the utilization of these. (8-9-97-BGC-1)

It then began explaining how I have difficulty in beginnings and endings of creative endeavors because of how I react to my own creations as they begin manifesting.

We see that this one has difficulty when the emotions become involved in this one's creative endeavors. We see that the degree to which this one moves the focus away from the creation at hand and directs it toward the emotional activity of the creation is the degree to which this one loses sight of the use of the understandings he possesses, the gaining of more understandings to add to the Self to become more complete, and the postponement of the manifestation of what it is that this one desires to produce. (8-9-97-BGC-1)

I knew this about myself in general, that I had a hard time getting going and a hard time completing things, but I had never thought I was reacting to my own creations. Why would I do such a thing?

The more I honestly examined this pattern, the more it all began to be clear. I had fears about my creations not being good enough, and so would be slow to start them. The ones I did begin, they would progress just fine until near the end, when I would again judge them as to their quality, and would often abandon them very close to the point of manifestation. I did this in just about every area of my life, too. I did this with relationships, jobs, projects in a job, schooling, artistic ventures, music productions. The scenes continued to pop up where I had done this to my creations. It was all-pervasive.

We see that this is true in all aspects of this one's life for we see that it is the emotions which are this one's major distraction at the present time, and we see that this has been a repeated pattern throughout this one's life. We see that there are times that the emotions are used in a conscious manner with awareness, but we see that more often this one expects the emotions to perform whatever function they need to and this one re-acts to the creation in the emotions rather than acting. We see that this would be changed by this one learning how to gain a perspective deeper than the emotions themselves. We see that this would begin by this one beginning to identify thoughts or concepts in regards to their creative potential rather than the feeling that they have, or bring, or stimulate. Would suggest that this one purposefully define experiences with all the senses. For in this way this one will become more cognizant of direct perception which is what this one desires. (8-9-97-BGC-1)

So what did I do as a result of this revelation? At first I was embarrassed and crushed. I felt like this was a pretty ingrained tendency, and that it would be too hard to change. But after a while, I found that I was beginning to be able to spot the reactions as they were happening in me.

We see that there is some difficulty in regards to the creative process. When this one initiates something new there is an inertia that this one seems to again and again need to overcome.

240

We see that this inertia is the manifestation of the lack of direction being given to what this one would understand as emotions. (8-9-97-BGC-1)

I could then say to myself, "Aha! I'm reacting to my own creation here. Hmm, let's see. I think that I'll go ahead and finish this, even though I think it's a failure (or silly or pointless)." Gradually, I got pretty good at seeing myself react, and choose a stronger finish to creations--doing them despite my sabotaging thoughts. It felt awkward, but it was working. I was achieving things I wanted instead of pushing them away at the last moment.

Would suggest to this one to begin to consider that the emotions are much more than what this one has given them credit for and they are much less powerful than what this one has given them credit for. They are merely one part of the expression of thought and as this one would begin to develop this kind of perception, there would be a great freedom that this one would have in not only using his creative abilities, but in also manifesting what this one images. This is all. (8-9-97-BGC-1)

I got the jobs I wanted, married the woman I wanted to, and made significant advances in my ability to lead as a teacher and director in branch Schools of Metaphysics.

My original Report also gave me another profound nugget of insight that I latched onto for years to come. It related that the areas where I could make the most progress in spiritual growth were in developing courage, security, autonomy and compassion.

You will also relate that which will foster a movement in the energy exchange between the ethereal and the material for the cultivation of genius.

Since the major disruption in the flow of creative energy within this one has to do with his emotional reactions to his creations, it would be of the greatest benefit in pursuing the fruition of creative potential and this one being able to become more cognizant of how this one utilizes the other creative parts of mind. We see that this one has a great capacity for expansive thinking and also to become very specific in identification. We see that the mastery of movement would aid this one greatly in being able to utilize more of the potential, to ease the experience of creation itself and to foster a deriving of deeper meaning to what it is that this one creates.

We see that this one very much uses the physical manifestation as a gauge for this one's creative ability. This is an inaccurate perception upon this one's part, for it is what this one has understood, what this one has added to the Self in regards to not physical things, but in regards to more spiritual things such as compassion, security, courage or autonomy. That is the reason why the creative process is even valuable to this one. It is in these four areas where this one can grow the most. This is all. (8-9-97-BGC-1)

When I heard those four areas, I knew I had a great gift of specificity. I now knew just where to focus my attention. I immediately went to work of assessing where I was with those qualities, and how to build them up. I found over time that in speaking up for the ideas I hold dear was the best way to include all of them. In being steadfast and true, loyal, to ideals I held, I built security and autonomy, and in speaking about them I built courage. It was through teaching what I have learned that I discovered compassion for others.

In 2002, as part of a class I was in, each student received a Creative Mind report. Since I had had one already in 1997, I was allowed a follow up question. I asked for a progress report and any further suggestions. The answer was positive, because I had been making progress with the suggestions, and it added something even more. It spoke of how I can unite my consciousness through using science and music principles. To a casual reader of the report that might be vague, but as a scientist musician I knew exactly what it was talking about. It was referring to how I approach problems scientifically, especially vibrationally, and how fascinated I am with the principles of resonance, which are included in science and music equally. Resonance is a key factor in a person's ability to cause rapid change, and I had even recently given a lecture on "Resonance and the Secret of Change".

The report ended with the suggestion that I explore the Power of Silence to gain the experience of unification of consciousness. A past life profile a few years ago had said I had built an understanding of the Power of Silence in a life as a Tibetan monk in which I explored the depths of sacred chanting seeking Oneness. I had that understanding inside me. That said to me that resonance is the way to explore unification as well as silence -- the Silence of Oneness.

It has only been recently that I made yet another break-through realization, based on my Creative Mind Report. I one day had the thought that maybe those four areas that the report had referred to--courage, autonomy, security and compassion--might in fact be understandings I have built and are within my consciousness, instead of weak areas in me that needed shoring up. That's why I could grow the most in those areas--because those were potential strengths, and I could use them to accelerate all areas of my life. That one thought vaulted me into a whole different way of seeing myself--that maybe I don't need all this fixing, but that I simply need to call more of myself forth in specific ways to accelerate my learning.

Through keeping this report and the follow up questions in my mind over several years, I have been able to advance my understanding of myself, of emotions, of understandings, and of self-value immensely. This report gives these suggestions to aid in cultivating genius, and I can see why and how it does. The report directly relates to being like the Creator, which is the principle reason we are all here in this earth plane. It gave me step by step instruction for how to be like the Creator, how and what I need to change to bring forth my genius, and specifics of using more of my understandings to accelerate my growth.•

A dreamschool Focus (following page) is an in-depth treatment of a dream topic. The one that follows is in response to a dreamer's email. The subject matter is the relationship between imagination and dreaming. This Focus includes excerpts from two books.

The Difference between
Night Dreaming and Conscious Imagery

Some time ago, a gentleman wrote asking for feedback on a meditation technique he tried. Here is his story and our response.

Hello,

I was looking for some one to help me interpret a bit of active imagination I experienced a while back.

Do you interpret this type of dream? A question first though: would you interpret this type of waking dream the same as a sleeping dream?

Ok I am trying to be specific, but I am not a psychologist neither do I meditate regularly. I only tried this out of curiosity, the meditation technique that is.

Experience: I was reading up on how to work into the active imagination. The instructions were guided to the point of suggesting that I should imagine my self in a cave with a door slightly off to the left. The procedure was to develop naturally by constructing these suggested surroundings until I was quite comfortable with letting my imagination take over. I was then to go through the door expecting to enter a spontaneous environment where I could meet an animal as a guide to introduce me to a spiritual guide or other archetype I might be interested in.

What I imagined spontaneously was an ice covered mountain top vista. I was naked cold and uncomfortable. Actually at that time I was looking to meet the archetype of the sun. Oh well! I also noted that the ice seemed to crack under my feet! I saw a snowy white and brown specked owl swoop into view. The owl led me to an eagle high in an

> *evergreen tree.*
>
> *Now I didn't see the eagle kill the owl or if the owl transformed into the eagle. However I was given a cloak made from the owl's feathers. The cloak was warm and I was comfortable again but at a loss as to what had just transpired. Then I came out of my session, about 25 minutes start to finish.*

Response

You describe your experience very well when you call it active imagination. We draw a distinction between day dreams and night dreams. The difference is easy to tell, day dreams originate in the conscious, waking mind and night dreams originate in the subconscious, inner mind.

What you describe we would call a guided imagery experience. The images you envisioned could be interpreted in dream symbology. However there are not the scientific conditions in place to indicate this would be an accurate interpretation. The truer meaning that might be derived from your experience would come from the context the instructions were given. In other words we could theorize and guess about your experience's meaning, and probably have a good deal of fun doing so, however you will gain more benefit by going back to the person who gave the instructions (be it a teacher, seminar leader, or author).

We teach progressive ways to explore and develop consciousness in our mastery of consciousness course. In fact there are ten essential life skills we teach in the first cycle of the course. These range from Self respect to concentration to creativity (imagination) to entrainment. Imagination is one of the ingredients of the power of the conscious mind which is reasoning. It is the element that allows for something different to occur than what has come before. This course is available at fourteen US cities and through correspondence. For more info contact som@som.org

The experience (and similar ones taught nowadays in magazines and books) you describe can be helpful in developing concentration, visualization, the reverie state, synesthesia, and intuitive senses. Since you really want to learn, it would be wise to find a teacher who has been where you want to go, one who has the heart and the head to guide you there.

*This gentleman might have benefited by reading the following excerpt from the book **Superconscious Meditation** by Dr. Daniel Condron.*

Meditation and the Mind
by Dr. Daniel Condron

The hour long meditation began first with a prayer, followed by deep breathing and a specific chant. In my prayer I asked to be close to the Creator. Shortly after starting the meditation, my mind became very still. Soon I felt a heaviness in my arms, as though they weighed 100 pounds. Then I reached a point where I felt myself moving within my body. I saw a dark tunnel, and I heard a voice telling me that I did have the capability to go to the inner levels. When the meditation ended, it took me longer than usual to bring my attention back to my physical body. I knew from that point forward that I could reach this state of freedom from the body whenever I desired.

It takes an investment to duplicate Kathryn's experience. Until you learn how to meditate you will spend most of your time in the Conscious Mind. The Conscious Mind is the division of mind associated with the brain, physical body, and five senses. The Conscious Mind will remain with you for only your lifespan on earth of 70 to 120 years or so.

The Subconscious Mind which is where the soul resides is permanent and will last as long as there is a single soul who needs to use it. All permanent learning which we may term understanding is stored in the individual's Subconscious Mind or soul. The temporary experiences you have this lifetime, the memories of experiences, and the sensory experiences will all be left behind at the end of this lifetime. What will remain is the you or the part of you that is eternal. The soul plus what you have gained this lifetime in the way of permanent understandings will remain as a part of you after this lifetime.

What determines if learning becomes understanding which then becomes permanent? For learning to be permanent, information must be reasoned with and found to be truth. Then the information, which has become knowledge through reasoning, must be applied in the life over and over until it becomes wisdom. Finally, the applied knowledge, called wisdom, must be taught to others so that the truth becomes a part of one's life. This is the process of producing understanding.

Meditation causes or creates an alignment of one's Conscious, Subconscious, and Superconscious Minds. The triangular effect in Diagram 1 represents the scattering of attention that occurs as I AM, which is the individuality and identity that is you, moves through the Superconscious Mind, Subconscious Mind and Conscious Mind. I AM exists in the physical and Conscious Mind as the conscious ego. Everyone is an I AM. Everyone existing in the physical experience has a conscious ego......

Different people use different nomenclature. You may have heard the term Universal Mind. You may ask, what is the difference between Universal Mind and Subconscious Mind?
Universal Mind is a term used to describe the quality of contraction of space, enhancement of communication and close connection that occurs in Subconscious Mind. In Subconscious Mind each of us has a mental hookup with everyone else, whether we use it or not. This mental or mind to mind connection is what makes telepathy possible.

When you have a telephone then you can phone a friend at a great distance. You can phone your parents. You can call your

248

brothers or sisters who live in a distant city. If you decide to phone someone then you need to know their telephone number. The same is true of using the interconnectedness quality of Subconscious Mind to perform mental or mind to mind communication. Telepathy only works when you know how to use it and you learn to use it by first disciplining your conscious mind.

As you delve deeper and deeper into meditation you will more and more experience this interconnectedness of yourself with other people and, in fact, all of creation. You will first discover and later come to know how to connect with others on a deeper level. You will come to know how to use your mental telephone to mentally contact any other person regardless of whether they are near you or halfway around the earth. (from **Superconscious Meditation** by Dr. Daniel Condron ©1998 School of Metaphysics)

....or this from Dr. Laurel Clark's **Shaping Your Life.**

Your Highest Ideals ... Man As Creator

Fairy tales, mythology, classic literature and history are filled with stories of miracles. Aladdin had a magic genie whose sole duty and purpose was to fulfill Aladdin's desires. King Midas received his wish to have everything he touched turn to gold. Hercules encountered many challenges and prevailed to win his desired rewards. Most children believe that when they throw a coin in a wishing well, blow out the candles on a birthday cake, ask Santa Claus or wish upon a star, their desires will be granted. All you have to do is decide what you want and your mind will work in magical and mysterious ways to give it to you. Your mind has the power to say to you, "Your wish is my command!"

Life can be an exciting adventure, a stimulating schoolroom, a world of experience which gives us opportunities to learn, to create,

249

and to prosper mentally, emotionally, materially, and spiritually. Every day we can awaken to the promise of enhanced awareness. How we create our life experiences and our world around us is determined by the degree of awareness we possess. The more we understand the purpose for life, the more enriched our everyday existence can be. The more we create the situations and circumstances we desire, the more we command the peace, contentment and happiness we deserve.

Years ago, when I was a young child of about five or six years old, I had a vision of the world as I imagined it could be. It didn't make sense to me that people were unhappy. It didn't make sense to me that people were mean, that they robbed or killed or hurt other people. I believed if people were truly doing what they wanted to do, then everyone would live in harmony and would be happy. I believed the source of such destructive actions was the unhappiness people experienced when they were living a life other than that which they desired. I thought that if someone was not doing what he or she wanted to do, he or she would take it out on other people by being nasty.

My vision was that each person knew him or herself. Everyone had a "calling," a vocation which was an expression of their true, inner heart's desire. As a result, everyone was content, and everyone reached out to give to one another. Because each person had his or her own unique talents and abilities, he or she was able to help other people who didn't have those abilities. The world was like a big puzzle, and each piece was a person who was fulfilling his or her heart's desires and creating from the depth of his or her being.

Although I have matured since that time, I still believe when an individual is doing what he or she truly desires to do, when he is creating from the source of his being, he is content. I have heard objections to this idea: "You're crazy! If everyone is running around doing whatever they please there will be chaos! People will kill one another! They will damage each other's property!" I have found this to be untrue. When someone creates, he fills his soul with awareness and understanding. If his creation benefits his soul, spiritual Self, or inner Self, it will benefit other people as well. People only hurt one another when they are denying their creative urge.

250

The lives of famous people illustrate this. Today we often take for granted the achievements of men and women who came before us. A person we call a "genius" is often one with a drive to pursue excellence. When one responds to the urge to reach within the depths of themselves and brings forth what they believe and know to be true, they are motivated by the highest passion. The people we remember are ones who gave themselves to life, who were always striving to reach higher, to delve deeper, to demand of themselves the best. Our lives are different because such people give; their influence spans generations.

Consider Shakespeare, whose understanding of universal truth and the nature of humanity has been passed down for centuries from the words of his pen. Or Euclid, who defined structure, and whose postulates and axioms form the basis of today's geometry although he lived in 300 B.C. Albert Einstein is another example of an individual whose creativity has influenced the entire world. Although he never did well in school, his curiosity about the universe led him to discover the principle of relativity and eventually the tremendous power of atomic reactions. Einstein believed in a God "who reveals himself in the harmony of all being" and his scientific research is a testimony to his drive to discover and know his own Creator.

Marie Curie, another scientist, overcame obstacles to bring the discovery of radioactivity to the world. Born in Poland during a time when education was forbidden to women, Curie travelled to France to attend the Sorbonne, and graduated first in her class with concentration in physics and mathematics, unheard of for women at the time. Her original intention was to become educated to teach so that she could bring about her vision of a free Poland. Her scientific discoveries led her down a different path, and through her dedication, research, and inquisitive thinking, we now have radiation therapy and a greater understanding of the structure of the atom. Thomas Jefferson had a similar dedication to education. Of his many achievements he considers the establishment of the University of Virginia to be his greatest. Jefferson was committed to a vision of insuring that each person be free to live up to the potential given to us by our Creator. The primary author of the Declaration of Independence, Jefferson believed that

251

"the God who gave us life gave us liberty" and through his actions ensured that the United States of America would provide a structure to enable its citizens to live this truth.

Leonardo da Vinci was another individual who was so full of talents he excelled in many diverse areas. An artist and sculptor, civil engineer, architect, military planner, inventor, scientist, and draftsman, in all of his activities he held a vision of a better life. He drew designs for a flying machine, the mechanics of which are used in aircraft today. Dissecting corpses and using his artistic genius, he drew the first anatomy textbook with accurate pictures of the human body. His ideas were so far ahead of their time that many were not made into machines during his day, but nonetheless he gave what he knew and had the courage to explore ideas that seemed crazy to those less enlightened than he.

There are many stories of men and women like these whose lives continue to touch ours generations later. These people have changed the world through their incessant search for truth, their drive and determination to find answers to the meaning of life, and their use of imagination, will power, and mental discipline. They were not born this way, they became this way through living lives of purpose and through keeping alive the inner voice of truth. The great American philosopher and writer Ralph Waldo Emerson said, "To believe your own thought, to believe that what is true for you in your private heart is true for all men, -- that is genius." When a person discovers a truth that has universal application and has the courage to communicate these ideas to the world, he or she makes a mark. Humanity progresses as a result of their desire and willingness to create a better world.

We each have an urge to create. We are happy when we are creating. Look at children. They are always inventing stories, designing clubs with rules and regulations of order, building houses with blocks, drawing, making up songs. Unfortunately, gradually and subtly children learn to squelch their creative drive. Adults tell them they need to be serious, to be practical. They hear in verbal and nonverbal ways, "You will never amount to anything. You're too idealistic! Don't expect too much and you won't be disappointed. Oh, that's just a pipe dream. Get real!" So, as we mature physically, we become stunted spiritually. We learn to turn down or even shut off our creative drive. We learn we can't have what we want.

Learning how to create, how to re-awaken the imaginative urge we are born with, starts with understanding that we are worthy. Why not have what we want? We each have free will, we each have intelligence and existence and the ability to reason. We have the means to be responsible for our choices. And we have a great power known as imagination. Every time we create, we become more aware of who we are and our capabilities. Every time we conceive an idea and bring it to fruition, we produce life. Unlike animals, as human beings who think and reason and imagine, when we create new life we also create awareness. We are life becoming aware of itself.

Benjamin Franklin is an excellent example of a man whose creative endeavors developed his Self awareness. Like Thomas Jefferson and Leonardo da Vinci, Franklin was truly a "Renaissance Man" of many talents -- a writer, editor, scientist, inventor, statesman, ambassador, publisher, printer, and philosopher. He is a remarkable figure whose optimism, sense of humor and practical wisdom have been handed down through proverbs like "Diligence is the mother of good luck." Franklin dedicated his life to the continual improvement of himself. In his autobiography he describes a life plan he devised for attaining perfection. Each morning, Franklin would arise and ask himself the question, "What good will I do today?" He identified thirteen virtues which he believed to encompass the human perfection he desired: temperance, silence, order, resolution, frugality, industry, sincerity, justice, moderation, cleanliness, tranquillity, chastity, and humility. Franklin chose one virtue a week to practice with diligence and recorded his progress daily. At the end of each day, he would review what he had learned, how he had evolved, and would ask himself the question, "What good did I do today?" and meditate upon this. Cultivating one virtue a week, practicing to develop it every day, Franklin repeated this cycle four times a year every year of his life. He was reportedly a very happy man, and attributed his happiness to this philosophy: "The most acceptable service to God is doing good to man."

Benjamin Franklin understood the principle that aiding others to abundance produces abundance in oneself. This example shows us that the secret to happiness does not lie in acquiring material things. We can use creative imagery for physical objects, to produce desired conditions, and to achieve status and recognition. The kind of creation that brings us the greatest joy, however, is that which brings us closer to our own creative essence. As we create, we discover more about our own wisdom, power, limitlessness, and originality. We learn what is infinite and eternal. We find out what links us with all of humanity, for we all emanate from the same origin. When we create for the purpose of understanding our own creative nature, we build security, for the laws of creation are just, immutable, and timeless. The thrill of connecting with that eternal source of creativity inspires us to strive to become the best we can be.• (from Shaping Your Life by Dr. Laurel Clark, copyright 1994, SOM.)

Dream of the Month Club members receive a case history of a dream containing common symbols and themes. The detailed interpretation is meant to aid members in becoming self-sufficient in understanding their dreams. The following is an in-depth treatment of a dream focusing on the dreamer's sense of value.

A dreamschool CASE HISTORY

Recently I became interested in dreams when I experienced three dreams of death, within a month's time. I hardly ever remember my dreams. These 3 dreams however, were very realistic. I remember what I had felt emotionally, what I was wearing, and exactly what I thought. At first I was extremely scared. Thinking I was going psychotic or something. They all dealt with death.

Then there was a fourth dream, that meant nothing at first. But becomes interchangeable with one of the death dreams. I did some research and sort of got the highlights. Any input you could offer would be wonderful. Actually doing a research paper for psychology, and would like to use my own experience with dreams as an example.

Dream # 1:
Was at work walking in the basement with one of my coworkers/ friend. We got onto the elevator as we were chatting. I got in first and her arm got stuck, but the elevator kept going, and she yelled out "don't worry about it, I will see you up there." But her arm was still in the elevator. I remember thinking. Man, her arm just got chopped off. I arrived on the second floor. (Where I usually work), got out of the elevator, and she wasn't there. Went up to the nurse's station where it was very dim, like at shift change. There were the other nurses receiving report. I told them what had happened. We went to the elevator. There she was. All chopped up into many pieces. I thought to myself. How did that happen? Then assumed she had been on top of the elevator, and crawled in through the crawl space. Her eyes were open and a leg here twisted, and an arm here. Then I stepped back and looked down the hallway and her mother was coming. She is employed there also. She is the director of nursing, my boss. I remember thinking, man, she can't see this. So I walked towards her. She kept coming. By the time we got to the elevator, there was nothing but a big bloody mess, streaks of it everywhere. But the body was gone. There stood the housekeeper w/a trashbag. Then I woke up.

Dream # 2:

I was in a coworkers house. I walked in without knocking. Passed this girl I never seen before, standing in the living room. She didn't say anything. I walked around in a circle looking for my coworker. Her boyfriend was there. He trapped me in the stairwell and began flirting with me. Then she approached and laughed about it. We all talked then began to leave the house, passing this girl, that still said nothing. We walked outside down to my car, we all got in. I looked over to my passenger seat and it was no longer my coworker, but my cousin. I started the car, looked up, and there was this big privacy fence, brownish colored, with these big red things on it. They were round, wet, and stringy. We got out to investigate. Upon walking closer to the fence it looked like organs of some sort. It was a stomach and intestines strung all over, hanging from this fence. A pool of blood lay in the dirt. No grass but all dirt. In this pool of blood lay a diamond ring. I picked it up, knowing whom it belonged to. Followed the blood trail to a maroon minivan, where there was her body all wrapped up in a white plastic bag and taped. It was another coworker. She doesn't even have a diamond ring. Then I woke up.

Dream # 3:

I just remember this one vaguely. All I know in this one is that my little brother had died. His car went over the rail into the water. He couldn't get the windows down and he drown.

Dream # 4:

My friend has a new boyfriend. He proposed to her. This ring he gave her was very distinct part of the dream. It was bronze colored. Had this covering, like metals doors that interlock, that open with switch on the side of it. The diamond is enclosed in this. Once opened, the most beautiful diamond I had ever seen is inside. We were just conversing then the dream went to that. That was all of it then.

Thank you so much for your time: Danielle in Ohio

256

SYMBOLS in the UNIVERSAL LANGUAGE OF MIND

Dream #1

work : represents how you are choosing to be productive in life to promote your growth and learning

hospital: indicates need for healing

basement: unconscious part of the mind

coworker/friend: when same sex, represents a familiar conscious aspect of the dreamer

elevator: means of movement between and to levels of consciousness

arm: purposeful intention

second floor: subconscious mind

nurses: familiar conscious aspects involved in healing

body pieces: body signifies mental attitudes of the dreamer

mother/boss: superconscious aspect

blood: life force, the truth

housekeeper: familiar conscious aspect

Dream #2

house: dreamer's mind

girl: unfamiliar conscious aspect, unconscious aspect

coworker: familiar conscious aspect

boyfriend: subconscious aspect

stairwell: means of moving between and to levels of consciousness

car: physical body

fence: a limitation in thinking

organs: stomach/intestines:

the body in a dream represents the mental attitudes of the dreamer. The stomach/intestines specifically

relate how the dreamer understands or assimilates his/her learning

blood: life force, truth

dirt: mind substance

diamond ring: value of commitment

minivan: physical body

another coworker's body: attitudes of dreamer

Dream #3
brother: familiar subconscious aspect
death: change
car: physical body
water: conscious life experiences
drowned: change

Dream #4
Friend: familiar conscious aspect
boyfriend: subconscious aspect
proposal: intent
ring: commitment
diamond: value

INTERPRETATION
in the Universal Language of Mind

We are glad you wrote and hope this will help you in your study as well as your growth. Many School of Metaphysics students have used aspects of what they learn in our classes as themes for papers and even as credit for independent studies of all types.

It is worth noting upfront that there are a series of people in your dream. Each represents an aspect of you. Same sex dream-people are aspects of your conscious, waking self. When you know them in your waking life, like the coworkers, they are familiar aspects that can easily be pinpointed by describing their outstanding attributes (efficient, pleasant, easygoing, harried, kind, arrogant, etc) that you also share. When the dream-people are of the opposite sex they signify aspects of your subconscious mind, your inner self or soul. You also have one superconscious aspect (the mother/boss) in your dreams. This shows you are experiencing in all three divisions of mind. What the experience is, is revealed by interpreting the dream action.

These four dreams are an arc within the month they occurred. Together they reflect a movement in consciousness, how your mind works and how you have changed, becoming more committed to

258

developing certain qualities. The transition is chronicled through four seemingly separate and unrelated dreams. When interpreted in the Universal Language of Mind the connections become clearer.

Dream #1 is set in a hospital which is a place of healing. This means your intention at the time of this dream was to see how things fit together. You were trying to understand the organic wholeness of something in yourself or your life. This was difficult for you because you were unaware of much of the process. This was symbolized by the beginning action in the basement. The dream was letting you know that there were things you might do or say with little conscious thought, either by habit or purely unconscious. The aspect of you symbolized by the coworker is linked to this tendency.

That aspect becomes very significant when her arm gets stuck in the elevator. This is an interesting image which pinpoints this part of you as the key to your intentions behind your acts. Your motivations are often conscious as you try to understand these patterns. You are separating and identifying what you have created or produced with your thoughts. (This is graphically symbolized by the body pieces.) This change in your awareness makes you more sensitive to your own authority, to what you know (the mother/boss), and you are willing to accept the truth about this. This could well signify that you are realizing you are the one to change and you determine when, who, and what.

In Dream 2 the scene is the coworker's house. Now you are ready to delve into how mind works. Dream 1 helped you see what your mind has produced. The difference between these two dreams is the difference between function and product. ie. Here's a working computer (dream 2), here's what can be created with it (dream 1). I n Dream 2 you are again making something conscious that has previously escaped your awareness. The clue is the unknown dream-girl doesn't say anything. This is your habit of not expressing your thoughts. The dream lets you know how this has affected your inner self (boyfriend) and this is progress for you. Recognizing this habit helps you further identify the unknown aspect in the dream-cousin. What do you and your cousin have in common? Identify that quality and you will know why you limit (fence) yourself. The dream tells you how you limit yourself, by refusing to assimilate what you learn. This is the symbology of the stomach and intestines on the fence. The stomach cannot function apart from the body. The dream shows that you believe assimilation is separate from motivation, purpose, mobility, creativity, intelligence, and all the mental attitudes the remainder of the body represents. The appearance of the body organs on the fence doesn't fit in the dream anymore than it would in waking life. But in the Universal language of Mind it tells you exactly what you need to know. There is value in you realizing this truth (the diamond in the blood) for the awareness changes how you see yourself.

Suggestion: When you assimilate knowledge you make it a part of yourself. This is brain entrained with the heart, functioning in more than the physical level alone.

In Dream 3 you have undergone another change resulting from manifesting your desires in your physical life. You are beginning to see how all along you have been getting what you want, even if you at times were unaware that you were asking for it.

By Dream 4, a new awareness has been brought into your subconscious mind, indicating that you are building understandings. You want to create anew and you are realizing on a new level what it will require to create what you desire. You determine what you want is worth it. This is symbolized by the most beautiful diamond you have ever seen.

Fitting the Dream into your Life

Together these dreams tell a story of your awareness over the short period of time that the dreams transpired. Every dream relates to the dreamer's conscious state of awareness and these dreams give you feedback on the changes you are making in who you are. It is possible that the dreams could be unrelated in terms of what they are addressing in your waking life, but since you are thoughtful, and

260

have already suspected connections, this is probably going to bear out. You will need to place the dream in the context of how you are choosing to live your life. These points will help you to this end:

1. Identifying the parts of you the dream-people represent will unlock the dream's meaning. Look for what you have in common with these people then you will be able to determine what part of you the dream is talking about.

2. Link the changes that have occurred to your waking state of thinking. By remembering what happened the days preceding the dream you will begin to see the thoughts and actions the dream was giving you feedback on. For instance with Dream 1 you will be looking for the ways you have become more consciously aware of your own motivations where before you were clueless.

3. Note the movement of dream-people from known females, to unknown female with boyfriend, to cousin, to your brother, to friend and her new boyfriend. This shows a progression in thought from unconscious, to conscious, to subconscious, to the desire for harmony between conscious and subconscious. This appears to be a growth cycle for you.

4. Be open to major situations (for example, at work or school, regarding family or relationships) that may be the issue these dreams are reflecting. The progression of thought the dreams indicate are probably linked to growth you have become increasingly aware of through this month.

Keep this in mind: In creating your life, your pattern has been to be unconscious of what motivates you ("I don't know why things turn out, they just seem to" or "if it's meant to happen it will happen" or "I didn't mean for things to turn out this way" or the like). This is changing as you are beginning to become more honest. You are paying closer attention to the connection between your thoughts and

261

what happens. You are identifying why things happen as they do. This has opened your awareness to how the mind works, and how you have placed limits on the abilities you possess. You have discovered the importance of assimilating what you are learning which in turn has led you to realize that commitment is more than just physical. It's more than keeping your word or being faithful to a cause. This idea has brought out into your conscious mind and changed some old ideas, those associated with your brother. This made way for a new pairing, a new use of your conscious and subconscious minds, with a deeper level of commitment than ever before for you.•

A dreamschool CASE HISTORY

STOLEN MONEY BUYS BACK CHILDHOOD
September 15, 2002 1:00 PM (wake up)

The dream starts out with Brit and I and two other friends (guy and a girl I have no idea who they are) hanging out. Brit and the guy friend go and rob a bank ($18,000 is stolen and for some reason I know that Brit has robbed a bank before when we've needed money.) Well they are concerned that they might in fact get caught so the four of us decide to go on the run and make a new start with the money we now acquired. We are in a truck and where ever we are going it takes 24 hours to get there. I miss my mom so much, (she has either died or is missing in the dream, but in real life she died 2 years ago of a heart attack) I hear from someone that she is back and I'm so happy.

I go to this hospital or something and there is my mom, she looks wonderful and is really thin (my mom was really about 300 lbs in real life). My sister is with her and tells me that my mom had had cancer and is better now and tells me that my mom made a line of fashion clothing (In real life I do not and never have gotten along with my sister, we hate one another). I decided to take my mom and sister with me on the trip. So I'm showing my mom and sister this 2 bedroom gorgeous water front condo that I apparently purchased (In real life I never seen this place before). I remember thinking, where are 6 people going to sleep in a 2-bedroom condo, and decided (In a childlike state or something) that girls will sleep in one room and boys will sleep in the other. I go put my 5 cats into a bedroom to let them settle in and so that we can unpack without them trying to escape outside.

Now all of the sudden my whole family (aunts, uncles, cousins, mom, dad, etc.) is gathered at a table for some sort of party or just some weird gathering (In real life I haven't talked to these people in 2 years). (The strange part is I'm now 10 years old (instead of 23) and everyone around me is the appropriate age of that same time frame (me being 10) but I'm still in the same condo. Suddenly my mom starts yelling at my uncle Jimmy about how poorly he has been treating me. They are fighting back and forth and then my uncle starts blaming everything on me. I jump in and yell that I haven't done anything wrong to him and that I try to keep in touch and remain close with him, so I ask him why he is lying to my face. He storms out saying he doesn't have to deal with this (In real life he would have reacted the same way.).

Now the condo morphs into a drivable condo and my mother begins chasing my uncle to resolve the conflict. The property now morphs to my grandmother's property (instead of the waterfront) as my mother continues her chase. My mom makes a really sharp turn and the house flips over and crashes. I run and check on everyone to make sure they are ok and then realize oh my god my cats. I get into the room they were in and I realize that there are eyeballs everywhere. All my cat's eyes are missing. I start freaking out crying and screaming at my mother about how much I hate her for this and how it is all her fault. Suddenly the condo morphs into my grandmother's old house. I find 2 cat cages and stuff my 5 cats into them to take them to a vet. Some strange black cat is in with my cats that I apparently gave to my mother.

My grandmother volunteers to take the cats and I to the vet. Before we leave I collect all the eyeballs and put them on a plate so the vet can reattach them but mixed in on the plate there are also cue balls for some unknown reason and there are 27 eyeballs and cue balls total. We leave for the vet and I'm still crying and feeling like we can't get there fast enough. We are having a hard time finding the vet. My grandmother is yelling at me for saying all those mean things to my mother. I explain that I didn't mean them and that I really love my mother (for some reason I know I'll never see my mother again). We reach the vet and I run my animals in and hand them the plate of eyeballs telling them to please reattach them. The nurse turns and for unknown reason says to me, "You should have used the stethoscope I gave you last time to monitor the cats, that's what I would have done because this one is better." The vet takes my cat and fixes them all with no problems.

I woke up feeling very detached and very sad. I have no idea what this dream means. The other strange thing about this is that I wrote my uncle (from the dream) like 6 weeks ago and he actually wrote me back today (email) and sent a picture.

S/female

SYMBOLS
in the UNIVERSAL LANGUAGE OF MIND

Brit : familiar conscious aspect of self
unknown male: unfamiliar subconscious aspect
unknown female: unfamiliar conscious aspect
bank: condition of mind where value is stored or exchanged
steal: attitude of taking from
truck: physical body of dreamer
mother: superconscious aspect
hospital: healing frame of mind
sister: familiar conscious aspect
cancer: attitude of hatred
clothing: how dreamer is expressing self
condo: house: mind
waterfront: conscious life experiences
sleep: loss of conscious awareness and will
cats: animals: compulsive ways of thinking, habits
family: familiar aspects of self
Uncle Jimmy: superconscious aspect
grandmother: superconscious aspect
eyeballs: tool for perception
vet: doctor: superconscious aspect
cue balls: game: perspective of life held by the dreamer
nurse: (female): unfamiliar conscious aspect
stethoscope: means to measure energy

INTERPRETATION
in the Universal Language of Mind

You are wrestling with how much it has been worth to you to complete something. You are trying to justify ideas of being taken from and this has several repercussions. Your body is working overtime, probably stressed out.

The value of what you have gone through is a greater love for self and a willingness to express your authority. This is a new attitude for you and it makes you feel more in control of your life. You still, however, feel that you lose something when you express what you really think. In an attempt to understand this you are looking at the value of being quiet, or holding back, and the value of speaking up. The reasoning you use in this evaluation process is habitual, the same that you always use.

You begin to trace this compulsive pattern back to when you were a kid. It's been with you a long time. The attitude that steals from you is being a victim. Whenever you feel out of control, like it doesn't matter what you say or do, you end up with the short end of the stick. This is a new thought for you and allows you a freedom you haven't had before. You feel more connected to what you know by realizing you are the one who has shortchanged yourself but this is a difficult reality to sustain. You are at a loss to relate your new perceptions with the old habitual ways of thinking. You don't understand why you couldn't "see" it all before.

The dream conveys the reason....because of emotional attachment to getting things over with.

Fitting the Dream into your Life

Have you recently finished something in your life? A job? A school year? A relationship? A project? Whatever fits into this category in your waking life is related to this dream. It also has a bearing on your sense of self worth and your health. Admit it has been worth it to complete this happening or circumstance in your life. Just because it may have brought out some unpleasant or even painful memories or emotions is not a good reason to dish the entire experience. In fact these surfacing thoughts and emotions are the mental clay to build a better sense of who you have become and who you can be.

This dream is about your authority, about how comfortable you are with what you know to be true. Although you have made some advances in how you express your authority, you are still holding onto the old way because it is comfortable and you are attached to it. Because of this, it is difficult for you to see things clearly. You want things to go back to the old way, and falsely believe if they do everything will be like it was.

266

It's kind of a Pandora's box.....you've already opened it and the truth has been perceived. Going back to the old way is not the answer. Build on what you know by strengthening your reasoning ability. By being willing to look for ways to emotionally mature, you will be free of the burden of childhood. Due to our karmic obligations to self, patterns establish themselves early in our lives. We become the shy one or the strong one or the boisterous one, and as we age parts of us grow to the neglect of others. This is a way we take from ourselves, not allowing our whole self to flourish and grow.

In some way you have recently become aware of doing this. Be willing to update your assessment of self. Learn to respond fully in the present rather than dredging up past hurts or disappointments. They may have no bearing on your present other than your own compulsive reaction pattern.

Instead of driving yourself to get things over with, begin perceiving completing what you begin as a journey, a process, that enables the real you to grow, evolve, express, learn. By consciously defining the purpose for your goals, you will find be able to give to yourself while you are giving to others. It is important to have a personal benefit in all you do. Create them.

Hope this gives you some direction. Congrats on reconnecting with your Uncle in your waking life. Forgiveness and love are powerful agents in our lives and they help us to remain fully in the present.•

Dreams

become a two-way communication when the conscious mind is willing to:

1] consciously register the message which comes in the form of a dream

2] consciously remember the dream

3] render the message, understanding its meaning

4] acknowledge the relevance of the message to your waking life

5] respond to what the subconscious mind has "said"

About the Author

Barbara Condron began exploring the meaning of her dreams at the age of six. Compelled to understand her dream experiences, she studied Christianity then psychology then metaphysics. She has discovered the point of origin where dreaming is both art and science. She has called dreaming the most commonly experienced form of intuition available to human beings. Dreams are the key for realizing the multidimensional nature of consciousness. Barbara teaches the development of consciousness, including lucid dreaming, at the College of Metaphysics. She lives on the campus of the college of Metaphysics with her husband Daniel and their son Hezekiah.

To find out more...

Since 1973, the School of Metaphysics has been aiding individuals to become whole, functioning Selves. Our course of study provides thought-provoking concepts and the spiritual disciplines to experience them. This is education as few have known it, education for Intuitive, Spiritual Man. From reasoning to intuition, from head to heart, from dreams to visions, from goal setting to total recall, mastering consciousness begins with Self respect and undivided attention. Our Mastery of Consciousness course is taught in fourteen Midwestern cities and the first level is taught through correspondence with a teacher at the College of Metaphysics.

The School of Metaphysics is a not-for-profit 501(c)3 educational organization. We invite those who want to spread our teachings to make a tax-deductible contribution.

Index

For home study...School of Metaphysics titles

Books

The Dreamer's Dictionary by Dr. Barbara Condron
Interpreting Dreams for Self Awareness
 by Drs. Laurel Clark and Paul Blosser
The Bible Interpreted in Dream Symbols
 by Drs. Condron, Condron, Matthes, Rothermel
Dreams of the Soul - The Yogi Sutras of Patanjali
 by Dr. Daniel R. Condron
Understanding Your Dreams by Dr. Daniel R. Condron
25 Most Commonly Asked Questions About Dreams
 by SOM Faculty

Books on Tape

Mechanics of Dreams by Dr. J. Rothermel $12.00
Dreams: Language of the Soul by J. Rothermel $8.00
Symbols of Dreams by J. Rothermel $12.00
Who are Those Strangers in My Dreams? by B. Condron $12.00

Audio Cassette Tapes ($8 each)

Using Dreams to Achieve Enlightenment by Dr. Daniel R. Condron
Five Steps of Creative Dreaming by Dr. B. Condron
Spiritual Science of Dreaming by Dr. Barbara Condron
Universal Language of Mind by Dr. Daniel Condron
Dreams: Inner Communication by Dr. Paul Blosser
Dreams & the Power of Subconscious Mind by Dr. D. Condron

Eight Lesson Audio Cassette Course

Dreamschool $40.00

Videos

Nocturnal Visions (VHS) $20.00
A World of Dreams (VHS) $20.00
The Science of Understanding & Interpreting Your Dreams
by Dr. Daniel Condron (DVD) $20

274

Additional titles available from SOM Publishing include:

The Wisdom of Solomon
Infinite Possibilities in Finite Experiences Book IV Infinite Being
Dr. Barbara Condron   ISBN: 0944386-33-4 $15.00

The Tao Te Ching Interpreted & Explained
Dr. Daniel Condron ISBN: 0944385-30-x $15.00

Peacemaking
9 Lessons for Changing Yourself, Relationships, & World
Dr. Barbara Condron   ISBN: 0944386-31-8 $12.00

How to Raise an Indigo Child
Dr. Barbara Condron   ISBN: 0944386-29-6 $14.00

Atlantis: The History of the World Vol. 1
Drs. Daniel & Barbara Condron ISBN: 0944386-28-8 $15.00

Karmic Healing by Dr. Laurel Clark   ISBN: 0944386-26-1
$15.00

The Bible Interpreted in Dream Symbols - Drs. Condron,
Condron, Matthes, Rothermel   ISBN: 0944386-23-7 $18.00

Spiritual Renaissance
Elevating Your Conciousness for the Common Good
Dr. Barbara Condron   ISBN: 0944386-22-9 $15.00

Superconscious Meditation
Kundalini & Understanding the Whole Mind
Dr. Daniel R. Condron   ISBN 0944386-21-0 $13.00

First Opinion: Wholistic Health Care in the 21st Century
Dr. Barbara Condron   ISBN 0944386-18-0 $15.00

The Dreamer's Dictionary
Dr. Barbara Condron   ISBN 0944386-16-4 $15.00

The Work of the Soul
Dr. Barbara Condron, ed. ISBN 0944386-17-2 $13.00

Uncommon Knowledge Past Life & Health Readings
Dr. Barbara Condron, ed. ISBN 0944386-19-9 $13.00

The Universal Language of Mind
The Book of Matthew Interpreted
Dr. Daniel R. Condron ISBN 0944386-15-6 $13.00

Permanent Healing
Dr. Daniel R. Condron ISBN 0944386-12-1 $13.00

Dreams of the Soul - The Yogi Sutras of Patanjali
Dr. Daniel R. Condron ISBN 0944386-11-3 $9.95

Kundalini Rising Mastering Your Creative Energies
Dr. Barbara Condron ISBN 0944386-13-X $13.00

To order write:

> School of Metaphysics
> World Headquarters
> 163 Moon Valley Road
> Windyville, Missouri 65783 U.S.A.

Enclose a check or money order payable in U.S. funds to SOM with any order. Please include $4.00 for postage and handling of books, $8 for international orders.

A complete catalogue of all book titles, audio lectures and courses, and videos is available upon request.

Visit us on the Internet at *http://www.som.org*
e-mail: som@som.org

276

About the School of Metaphysics

We invite you to become a special part of our efforts to aid in enhancing and quickening the process of spiritual growth and mental evolution of the people of the world. The School of Metaphysics, a not-for-profit educational and service organization, has been in existence for three decades. During that time, we have taught tens of thousands directly through our course of study in applied metaphysics. We have elevated the awareness of millions through the many services we offer. If you would like to pursue the study of mind and the transformation of Self to a higher level of being and consciousness, you are invited to write to us at the School of Metaphysics World Headquarters in Windyville, Missouri 65783.

The heart of the School of Metaphysics is a four-tiered course of study in mastering consciousness. Lessons introduce you to the Universal Laws and Truths which guide spiritual and physical evolution. Consciousness is explored and developed through mental and spiritual disciplines which enhance your physical life and enrich your soul progression. For every concept there is a means to employ it through developing your own potential. Level One includes concentration, visualization (focused imagery), meditation, and control of life force and creative energies, all foundations for exploring the multidimensional Self.

Experts in the Universal Language of Mind, we teach how to remember and understand the inner communication received through dreams. We are the sponsors of the National Dream Hotline®, an annual educational service offered the last weekend in April. Study centers are located throughout the Midwestern United States. If there is not a center near you, you can receive the first series of lessons through correspondence with a teacher at our headquarters.

For those desiring spiritual renewal, weekends at our Moon Valley Ranch offer calmness and clarity. Spiritual Focus Weekends center around a theme – kundalini, genius, meditation, influence – or explore marriage, parenting, or your purpose in life. Each includes an intuitive report designed for the session and given in your presence.

277

Mentored by College instructors and Psi counselors, these weekends are experiences in multidimensional awareness.

The Universal Hour of Peace was initiated by the School of Metaphysics at noon Universal Time (GMT) on October 24, 1995 in conjunction with the 50th anniversary of the United Nations. We believe that peace on earth is an idea whose time has come. To realize this dream, we invite you to join with others throughout the world by dedicating your thoughts and actions to peace through reading the Universal Peace Covenant as ONE VOICE at midnight December 31st. Living peaceably begins by thinking peacefully. Please contact us about how you can participate.

There is the opportunity to aid in the growth and fulfillment of our work. Donations supporting the expansion of the School of Metaphysics' efforts are a valuable way for you to aid humanity. As a not-for-profit publishing house, SOM Publishing is dedicated to the continuing publication of research findings that promote peace, understanding and good will for all of Mankind. It is dependent upon the kindness and generosity of sponsors to do so. Authors donate their work and receive no royalties. We have many excellent manuscripts awaiting a benefactor.

One hundred percent of the donations made to the School of Metaphysics are used to expand our services. Donations are being received for Project Octagon, the first educational building on the College of Metaphysics campus. The campus is located in the beautiful Ozark Mountains of Missouri. This proposed multipurpose structure will include an auditorium, classrooms, library and study areas, a cafeteria, and potential living quarters for up to 100 people. We expect to finance this structure through corporate grants and personal endowments. Donations to the School of Metaphysics are tax-exempt under 501(c)(3) of the Internal Revenue Code. We appreciate any contribution you are free to make. With the help of people like you, our dream of a place where anyone desiring Self awareness can receive wholistic education will become a reality.

We send you our Circle of Love.

278

The Universal Peace Covenant

Peace is the breath of our spirit. It wells up from within the depths of our being to refresh, to heal, to inspire.

Peace is our birthright. Its eternal presence exists within us as a memory of where we have come from and as a vision of where we yearn to go.

Our world is in the midst of change. For millennia, we have contemplated, reasoned, and practiced the idea of peace. Yet the capacity to sustain peace eludes us. To transcend the limits of our own thinking we must acknowledge that peace is more than the cessation of conflict. For peace to move across the face of the earth we must realize, as the great philosophers and leaders before us, that all people desire peace. We hereby acknowledge this truth that is universal. Now humanity must desire those things that make for peace.

We affirm that peace is an idea whose time has come. We call upon humanity to stand united, responding to the need for peace. We call upon each individual to create and foster a personal vision for peace. We call upon each family to generate and nurture peace within the home. We call upon each nation to encourage and support peace among its citizens. We call upon each leader, be they in the private home, house of worship or place of labor, to be a living example of peace for only in this way can we expect peace to move across the face of the earth.

World Peace begins within ourselves. Arising from the spirit peace seeks expression through the mind, heart, and body of each individual. Government and laws cannot heal the heart. We must transcend whatever separates us. Through giving love and respect, dignity and comfort, we come to know peace. We learn to love our neighbors as we love ourselves bringing peace into the world. We hereby commit ourselves to this noble endeavor.

Peace is first a state of mind. Peace affords the greatest opportunity for growth and learning which leads to personal happiness. Self-direction promotes inner peace and therefore leads to outer peace. We vow to heal ourselves through forgiveness, gratitude, and prayer. We commit to causing each and every day to be a fulfillment of our potential, both human and divine.

Peace is active, the motion of silence, of faith, of accord, of service. It is not made in documents but in the minds and hearts of men and women. Peace is built through communication. The open exchange of ideas is necessary for discovery, for well-being, for growth, for progress whether within one person or among many. We vow to speak with sagacity, listen with equanimity, both free of prejudice, thus we will come to know that peace is liberty in tranquillity.

Peace is achieved by those who fulfill their part of a greater plan. Peace and security are attained by those societies where the individuals work closely to serve the common good of the whole. Peaceful coexistence between nations is the reflection of man's inner tranquillity magnified. Enlightened service to our fellowman brings peace to the one serving, and to the one receiving. We vow to live in peace by embracing truths that apply to us all.

Living peaceably begins by thinking peacefully. We stand on the threshold of peace-filled understanding. We come together, all of humanity, young and old of all cultures from all nations. We vow to stand together as citizens of the Earth knowing that every question has an answer, every issue a resolution. As we stand, united in common purpose, we hereby commit ourselves in thought and action so we might know the power of peace in our lifetimes.

Peace be with us all ways. May Peace Prevail On Earth.

created by teachers in the School of Metaphysics 1996-7

280